BUT I DON'T SPEAK SPANISH

BUT I DON'T SPEAK SPANISH

A Narrative Approach to Ministry with Young People

Vincent A. Olea

FOREWORD BY Allan Figueroa Deck, SJ

Paulist Press
New York / Mahwah, NJ

Cover image by s_maria/Shutterstock.com
Cover and book design by Lynn Else

Library of Congress Cataloging-in-Publication Data
Names: Olea, Vincent A., author.
Title: But I don't speak Spanish : a narrative approach to ministry with young people / Vincent A. Olea ; foreword by Allan Figueroa Deck, SJ.
Description: New York : Paulist Press, 2019. | Includes bibliographical references.
Identifiers: LCCN 2018042349 (print) | LCCN 2018055867 (ebook) | ISBN 9781587687853 (ebook) | ISBN 9780809154081 (pbk. : alk. paper)
Subjects: LCSH: Church work with youth—Catholic Church. | Hispanic American youth—Religious life. | Church work with Hispanic Americans—Catholic Church. | Storytelling—Religious aspects—Christianity.
Classification: LCC BX2347.8.Y7 (ebook) | LCC BX2347.8.Y7 O33 2019 (print) | DDC 259/.2—dc23
LC record available at https://lccn.loc.gov/2018042349

ISBN 978-0-8091-5408-1 (paperback)
ISBN 978-1-58768-785-3 (e-book)

Published by Paulist Press
997 Macarthur Boulevard
Mahwah, New Jersey 07430
www.paulistpress.com

Printed and bound in the
United States of America

"Of all the trails in this life, there is one that matters most.
It is the trail of a true human being.
I think you are on this trail and it is good to see."

—*Dances with Wolves* (1990)

To my son, Andrew, and the generations that walk with him
upon the trail of a true human being. It is good to see.

Contents

Foreword ix

Acknowledgments xiii

Introduction xvii

I. NARRATIVE AND SALVATION IN MINISTRY 1

1. But I Don't Speak Spanish (My Story) 3

2. Proposing a Narrative Approach to Ministry with
   Young People 21

3. The Salvific Nature of Being Human 32

II: SALVIFIC NARRATIVES IN THE LIVES OF HISPANIC
   YOUNG PEOPLE 45

4. The Identity Narratives 49

5. The Generational Narratives 61

6. The Language Narratives 72

7. The Transformative Narratives 81

CONTENTS

III. PRACTICAL STRATEGIES FOR A NARRATIVE APPROACH TO MINISTRY 97

8. Strategies to See and Give Voice in a Narrative Approach ...99

  Strategy #1: Trust the Salvific Essence Alive in
            Young People 100

  Strategy #2: *See* How Young People Are Connected and
            Disconnected 101

  Strategy #3: Can We Just Stop Talking? 106

  Strategy #4: Give Voice Always and Everywhere 109

  Strategy #5: Convert Statements into Questions. 115

  Strategy #6: Name the Salvific Themes We See 116

9. Bringing Narratives Together by Bringing Lives Together... 119

  Strategy #7: Participate in Movement and Continue the
            Narrative............................... 120

  Strategy #8: Foreground the Hidden Narratives 125

  Strategy #9: Dialogue between Generations 129

10. The Animation of Sacred Space 133

  Strategy #10: Continue the Narratives in Hispanic
            Catholic Popular Religiosity 134

  Strategy #11: Create Ritual Experiences 140

  Strategy #12: Inspire Transformative Responses Using
            Scripture 148

Notes 163

Foreword

I met Vince Olea more than ten years ago at Barry University where he was a doctoral student in ministry taking my course on the pastoral care of Latino/as. Since then, I have had several opportunities to meet and speak with him at national and regional gatherings of ecclesial leaders. I would be hard-pressed to name a more experienced, thoughtful, or creative youth and young adult minister in our country today. *But I Don't Speak Spanish* is the fruit of Vince's vast experience and study. It is extremely timely, coming as it does on the heels of the second synod convened and organized under the reform-minded papacy of Pope Francis, the Fifteenth Ordinary General Assembly of the Synod of Bishops, on the theme "Young People, the Faith, and Vocational Discernment."

Vince has marvelously integrated several key elements of a solid approach to youth and young adult ministries: (1) the vast riches of his own life struggles and stories, (2) a healthy humanistic psychology, (3) years of in-depth experiences of serving the Church and civil society in the human and spiritual formation of youth, and (4) a substantial background in and passion for theological learning. The result is impressive, indeed. It is an easy read even though it deals with complex and weighty developmental issues and provides many insights of both a practical and conceptual nature. Every chapter comes alive with the author's wide-ranging professional praxis, as well as with insights culled from his reading of the scriptures, of key theologians, and spiritual writers.

The meat of this book resides in the sustained and coherent way Vince applies insights about the nature and role of storytelling—narrative—throughout the book. He explores and develops narrative as a most effective method for addressing challenges facing the formation of youth and young adults. In particular, the book addresses today's dramatically shifting intercultural and generational contexts that demand flexibility and more than a one-shoe-fits-all mentality. Vince differentiates among the generations served today and provides a way forward for today's and tomorrow's ministers grounded in a narrative methodology and a Vatican II and Pope Francis vision of the human person in relation to a loving, merciful God. In all this, Vince focuses, of course, on Latino/a youth and young adults who constitute the majority of Catholic youth and young adults in the United States today. His reflections, nevertheless, are not limited to U.S. Latino/as since many of his insights and methods are pertinent to other cultural groups in the hyper-pluralist and diverse contexts of our country.

But I Don't Speak Spanish is especially significant considering the ways in which it exemplifies the core insights of the reform Pope Francis is striving to bring about in the Catholic Church today. At the center of this vision is a Christian anthropology that insists on God's nearness, tenderness, and mercy. Vince reveals a deep regard for the trinitarian theology of Catherine LaCugna who provided the groundwork for this vision in *God for Us*, where she distills a lifetime of research and writing on the mystery of the Blessed Trinity. She stresses the significance of those three words: *God for us*. She makes the point that the Christian understanding of a trinitarian God must conclude that this God is loving, tender, and merciful, in contrast to other renditions of the theological tradition that have wittingly or unwittingly left Christians and others with the idea of a judgmental and fearsome deity. Pope Francis proposes what some commentators have called a "revolution of mercy." He has attempted in multiple ways to reframe our understanding, image, and attitude toward God in a way that begins and ends with his mercy, period. Vince demonstrates the profound implications of this for the various moments of human, faith, and spiritual formation in people. Telling our stories and integrating them and our lives into the biggest narrative of all—God's radical demonstration of his love for us in the incarnation—is the human project. This "big picture" translates into a life of mindfulness, prayer, and discerning love in action that provides wholeness and healing to our otherwise limited and usually fragmented stories.

Foreword

Vince Olea provides us with a poignant, heartfelt, and personal memoir, a primer of sorts on practical theology, and an inspiring spiritual journal all in one. Enjoy!

Allan Figueroa Deck, SJ
Distinguished Scholar of
Pastoral Theology and Latino Studies
Loyola Marymount University
June 25, 2018

Acknowledgments

Beyond the years of work in ministry, study, and writing, many wonderful people have made this book possible. All have contributed to the stories, theological insights, and ministerial proposals within the book. I am eternally thankful and honored to have encountered each:

My beloved family: Patty, Andrew, Angela, Mom (Madeline), Dad (Eugene), Mike, Bea, Stephanie, Chris, Margaret, Filomena, Eugene, Heather, Sarah, Vance, Sonia, Miguel, Frank, Linda, Melissa, Michael, Jessica, Nixon, and Madix.

My mentors and theological companions: Daniel Christopher, J. Gordon Nelson, Richard Rohr, OFM, Allan Deck, SJ, Tim Matovina, Tammara Moore, Jorge Moreno, Patty Jimenez, Rudy Vargas IV, Hilda Mateo, Francisco Castillo, Alicia Marill, Jorge Presmanes, OP, Mark Wedig, OP, Elsie Miranda, Gloria Schaab, SSJ, Wayne Cavalier, OP, Sara Fairbanks, OP, Thomas Rausch, SJ, Lily Roggenkamp, Cece Aguilar, MP Bausch, Angie Maloney, Cami Kasmerchak, and Marie Stone.

My companions at Dolores Mission: Jane Argenta, Yolanda Brown, Leon Brown, Rosa Campos, Rita Chairez, Teresa Collier, Karina Moreno Corgan, Emily Diaz, Leonard Diaz, Jessenia García, Marisol García Macías, Norma Gillette, Juanita Guillan, Ellie Hidalgo, Alma Islas, Gilberto Lomeli, Yecenia Lomeli, Arturo Lopez, Eddie Martinez, Freeman Michaels, Jasmine Michaels, Mark Potter, Amy Rios, Carlos Rodriguez, Raquel Roman, Yesenia Salcido, Cynthia Sanchez, Jana Sosnowski, Scott Santarosa, SJ, Stephen Corder, SJ, Sean Carroll, SJ, Joe Speiler, SJ, Greg Boyle, SJ, Robert Dolan, SJ, and Shannon Smith.

My companions, the Youngsters at Dolores Mission: Eleesa Avila, Gloria Avila, Oscar Avila, Belen Aguilar, Evelyn Aguilar, Giovanni

Aguilar, Jonathan Aguilar, Liz Aguilar, Randy Aguilar, Erik Baires, Natalie Coleman, Jerry Escobar, Tony Escobar, David Estrada, Robert Dolan, SJ, Jesus Toño García, William Mathias, Omar Perez, Teresa Portillo, Luis Rios, Alex F. Rodriguez, Mauricio Roque, Betty Villalba, and Nestor Villalba.

My companions at Santa Teresita Youth Conference Center: Bishop John Steinbock, Cristal Juarez-Garcia, Migdalia Vasquez, Alfredo Camarena, Alejandro Barraza, Elaine Bauer, Savannah Boiano, Ingrid Borja, Danny Braia, Roxanne Cano, Brenda Cayente, Andrea Chavez, Ramon Chavez, Fr. Rod Craig, Ruby de la O, Gilberto Garcia, Darrilyn Durr, Rick Durr, Marcos Espinoza, Rosy Esteves, Mike Hand, José Garcia, Gilberto Garcia, Marco Garcia, Tim Garner, Stan Gold, Ruby Gomez, Isaias Gonzalez, Karla Gonzalez, Fr. John Griesbach, Edgar Guzman, Bill Heisdorf, David Hernandez, Kathi Hernandez, Rose Hernandez, Barbara Lahmann, Fr. Mike Lastiri, Brenda Limon, Arturo Lopez, David Lynch, Abraham Magaña, Lucy Magdaleno, Gabriel Maldonado, Candy Maldonado, Adan Madrigal, Darlene Mayfield, Antonio Miranda, Martha Miranda, Roxanne McWilliams, Salvador Martinez, Ruben Mejia, Yvette Mejia, Alicia Meza, Isaac Meza, Jessica Palomera, Justin Palomera, Jorge Perez, Diana Ramirez, Monica Rodriguez, Noemi Rodriguez, Samantha Rodriguez, Ashley Rosales, Ana Salazar, Mike Salinas, Yesco Standfree, James Tasy, Dorie Talob, Victor Torres, Hanya Tovar, Julia Valtierra, Andrea Vasquez, Dave Vasquez, and Sr. Daniel Witt.

My companions at St. John the Evangelist: Carrie Baranowski, Annie Beiner, Carrie Beiner, Jane Beiner, Marita Beiner, Anastasia Billings, Justin Breen, Brian Brown, Andy Corrao, Brian Carroll, Gregory Carroll, Tim Carroll, Brian Casey, Jimmy Cea, Rocco Cimarusti, John Clark, Dana Clyman, Meaghan Cosgrove Alvarez, Cory Cosgrove Garcia, Elizabeth Decker, Nick DeFilippis, Claire Deken, Holly Holeva Deken, Isaac Deken, Hugh Deken, Nat Deken, Robin DuBroy, Christy Feehan, Nicole Feehan, Kathleen Feehan, Laura Fernandez, Cynthia Garrity-Bond, Catherine Gorey, Katie Grosse, Msgr. Timothy Harnett, Nicole Hill, Ashley Jenks, Kurt Jordan, Taryn Keenan, Tami Kelly, Kerry Kelly-Cochrane, Dolores King, Julie Koopmans, Valerie Lieberman, Lauren Logan,

Acknowledgments

Jeremy Long, Rachel Lopez, Lauren Lyon, Desireé Martinez, Ben McGuire, Victoria McGrath, Joanie Mendenhall-Lefkowits, Mary Anne Mendenhall, Katherine Mendenhall, Mary Moffett, Trudi Morgan Saltamachio, Gabby Obeji, Ann Pattison, Brook Pattison, Craig Pattison, Matt Peacock, Jacy Pedry-Edwards, Wendy Pepper, John Pini, Cindy Prieto, Jesse Ramirez, Jeff Reid, Deeva Rivera, Monica Rivera, Andy Scheafer, Mike Scharbarth, Abby Shull, Andi Shull, Anthony Silvas, Marissa Silvas, Sonia Silvas, Sherrie-Anne Stacy, Lauren Stevenson, Ludo Vincent, Becky Voaklander, John Wilcsek, and Ashley Williams.

Introduction

The primary function of ministry is to uncover and nurture the salvific narratives in the lives of the people of our communities.

This book is about God being alive in our human existence, and then what that means for Christian ministry. Imagine ministry entrenched in everyday life, engaging everything as if it were part of life's grand narrative, *God with us and for us.* How intriguing to propose an approach to ministry that places this human-Divine reality at the forefront.

The intrigue, of course, is not in the proposal but in an approach built upon what God has created in humanity: our innate salvific essence that reverberates into every sliver of human life and dances between our painful experiences of alienation and our beautiful encounters with each other and God.

To be sure, this viewpoint is not new but echoed over time. We hear it in Paul's Letter to the Colossians: "For in him all things in heaven and on earth were created, things visible and invisible….He himself is before all things, and in him all things hold together" (Col 1:16–17). We hear it in the words of St. Irenaeus, "The glory of God is a human being fully alive." We hear it in Richard Rohr's mantra "Everything belongs." Similarly, in ministry, this viewpoint is recognized in the centrality of Jesus's ministry to those on the periphery, in contextual approaches born out of Catholic social teaching, and in the notion of *lo cotidiano*, the everyday reality where life and salvation are made known. It follows that what I propose is not new but rather a continuation of thought and praxis invested in everyday life, especially the lives of young people.

From within the depth of this human context, narratives appear like puzzle pieces representing the parts and fragments of our lives, which are linked or long to be linked to other narratives. These narratives appear lifewide and lifelong, and they consciously and unconsciously long to be voiced, heard, touched by, and united to others and to God. They are salvific for that very reason. It is within this paradigm that we will uncover and nurture the salvific narratives as the fundamental function of ministry.

Out of this narrative perspective, pastoral leaders are summoned to see and nurture the salvific pieces and fragments hidden and expressed in the totality of the lives of young people. This happens as we step into the unique narratives of their everyday lives, those that are personal, cultural, generational, relational, psychological, local, somatic, hidden, unconscious, unclean, unjust, religious, communal, and global. Such narrative pieces constitute the dimensions that define and shape who they are, which deserve the full attention and empathic engagement of pastoral leaders.

Other narrative pieces need attention, especially those that are not typically considered Christian but possess a salvific quality, as most dimensions of our lives do. In addition to the hidden and unclean dimension, these include the broken, alienating, arousing, secretive, creative, bodily, aggressive, sexual, rebellious, insatiable, subversive, and misunderstood dimensions, just to name a few. All are sacred, as all things human carry a salvific theme or glimmer. Each contributes to the human condition, the created space where God lives, the space where the "shit" of life happens—the places, the parts, and the spaces where God is most evident, most alive, and most needed.

Naturally, ministry is defined from many viewpoints, and effective ministry involves a myriad of components. However, each emphasis, from communal worship, to catechesis, to social justice, and to sacramental engagement is brought to life as pastoral leaders give voice to and interact with the everyday salvific narratives of young people. This way of thinking about ministry is especially relevant today since so many young people are disassociated from institutional religion. By moving ministry from church space to human space, pastoral leaders enter more deeply into the human landscape of young people, and by doing so, enter into a world filled with evidence of God's saving grace.

Ultimately, by emphasizing everyday human life, we transform the agenda of "get 'em to the pews" by first seeing how God is already alive in the lives of young people, whether they themselves recognize it or not. As we witness the fundamental presence of God in their lives, we become the ones affected by young people, transformed by their broken beauty. Through these encounters, our Christian proclamation takes a turn inward and we are then able to proclaim our most fundamental Christian utterances from their sacred spaces, from their lived realities. Through these encounters, *we experience the good news*: that God is always with us, always for us, and never abandons us…always and everywhere no matter what.

The ubiquitous reality of God with us translates into a narrative approach that applies to all ages and cultural contexts. However, in presenting this approach, we emphasize its value within three contexts: young people, Hispanic culture and ministry, and my experiences as a Hispanic pastoral leader serving 1.5-, second-, and third-generation Hispanic young people.

Within this contextual framework, this narrative approach is uniquely capable of responding to the growing Hispanic Catholic population in the United States. With 36 million Hispanics at a median age of nineteen years old and born in the United States, it is no surprise that most young Catholics today are Hispanic. Reports also tell us that young Hispanics are the largest ethnic population of young people disassociated from religious institutions today. These growing realities demand new ways of doing ministry so that we can move more deeply into the lives of these young Hispanics to contribute to their growth, healing, faith development, and transformation.

As pastoral leaders step into the lives of Hispanic young people, we cannot help but engage narrative themes related to language, culture, migration, immigration status, religious traditions, identity, discrimination, exile, family, community, and social justice. Given this array of narrative dimensions, stepping into this sphere may be intimidating for those who do not speak Spanish and for those who are not Hispanic. Yet, as the composition of Hispanic identity widens to include a bilingual majority, and the identity of those who serve Hispanic youth expands to reflect pastoral leaders who are not Hispanic, our function as pastoral leaders remains that of uncovering and nurturing the salvific narratives in the everyday lives of the young people we serve. This book presents narrative examples, personal stories, biblical insights, and twelve key practical strategies to serve our faith communities in our walk with the young people we serve.

In this spirit of connectivity and inclusion, the title for this book is *But I Don't Speak Spanish*. These words represent my reality as a third-generation Mexican American who does not speak Spanish. This reality appears as an identity marker in my life connecting me to how I practice ministry.

But I Don't Speak Spanish also reflects the dynamic interconnection between language, culture, and identity, and the challenges in navigating these dimensions especially for the growing number of bilingual and monolingual (English) Hispanic young people today. Consequently, such important narrative themes emerge through their in-between existence at work and the need for us to uncover and nurture them.

Finally, for those new to Hispanic ministry, the title, *But I Don't Speak Spanish*, equally represents an invitation to consider your narrative dimensions and those of the young people in your communities as part of our ongoing connectivity espoused by this approach. Thus, we are assured that we all belong and contribute to the human salvific partnership we share.

Part I

❧·❦·❧

NARRATIVE
AND SALVATION
IN MINISTRY

1

But I Don't Speak Spanish (My Story)

My name is Vincent Andrew Olea and I am third-generation Mexican American...*but I don't speak Spanish*. This is my story.

Living on opposite sides of the United States-Mexico border, my maternal grandparents began their romance as teenagers, my grandmother, *Manuela Ruiz*, from Agua Prieta, Sonora, in Mexico, and my grandfather, *Alfredo Dela Vara*, from Douglas, Arizona. For both, Spanish was their primary language. They married in 1938 in Douglas, where my mother was born in 1940.

My mom grew up in Boyle Heights, California, and my dad, also of Mexican descent, grew up in nearby East Los Angeles. For both my parents, Eugene and Magdalena Olea, Spanish was also their first and primary language growing up.

My dad tells stories of the ridicule and physical abuse he endured as a little boy at the hands of his peers due to his thick Mexican accent. He also recalls getting his hands slapped by his kindergarten and first-grade teachers for speaking Spanish in the classroom. By the second grade, his English had improved, however, his accent remained and so, too, did the humiliation. Those early years were so traumatic that my dad developed a speech impediment. He would clench his teeth shut when he spoke, and it took years of work with a Vincentian priest for him to recover.

My dad also spoke of *a culture of violence* in his family, and I believe that the intermingling of family violence and the humiliation

3

he experienced over his Mexican accent contributed to his desire to separate from *his* past, because he didn't want those painful experiences to be ours, his kids.

For my mother, though, the absence of Spanish in our household did not symbolize a separation from the past, as with my dad, but was connected to her hope for the future—living the American dream.

My parents got married in 1961 and quickly made many babies. I am the second of five, was born in 1963, and grew up thirty miles from downtown Los Angeles. Both my parents worked hard to advance in their careers, my dad as a hospital administrator and my mom as a county social worker, both earning master's degrees.

Having dropped out of high school, it was my grandmother's promotion of a middle-class dream that inspired my mother to work hard and persist through experiences of financial hardship. My mother, too, desired for all of us to live a middle-class life, which meant education, family, career, home, and opportunity.

We grew up as good obedient Catholics of simple means, and although Spanish was not spoken in our home, our Mexican culture was evident in our family life, in our Catholicism, in our love for the Blessed Virgin Mary, in our Christmas traditions, and in our food—beans and tortillas were a family staple (which is my favorite food today). In fact, in 1969, I believe I was the first person to create a peanut butter and jelly burrito, although I have no evidence to prove it.

Several years after my breakthrough in *mestizo* burrito making, I had my first experience of God in a movie theater watching *Jesus Christ Superstar*. I was nine. I left the movie theater dripping wet with emotion and presence, and I spent the entire thirty-minute ride home lying weeping in the back-storage section of our family VW bug.

On reflection, I have unconsciously spent my adult life trying to understand the salvific meaning of that night as the first of many powerful, symbolic, and somatic encounters with the Divine, which have occurred in the most human of circumstances.

But I Don't Speak Spanish

❦ ⸙ ❧

My son, Andrew, was born in 1985, when I was twenty-one, and it was his birth that inspired me to return to school and the Church. Andrew's mother and I never married, which meant that most of his young life was spent in two households raised by two young single parents.

In 1996, feeling the pain of my shortcomings as a father, and inspired by Richard Rohr's work with men and my own study of initiation rites, I unconsciously summoned my Mexican sense of ritual, symbol, affect, and drama (which is so evident in the rich popular religiosity of Mexican culture) and created an initiation rite for my son that involved four generations of men—my grandfather, father, me, and my son. It also involved a Franciscan priest, Fr. Rusty, and took place on the eve of Andrew's eleventh birthday (Ash Wednesday) at midnight at the Mission San Luis Rey in Oceanside, California.

The purpose of the rite was to initiate Andrew into his journey as an emerging man. On a deeper level, the rite was a way for us to be-in-relationship. It was a promise that we are accompanied by our God and each other, and a hope that together we will live this grand reality. While the details of that night are beyond the scope of this book, there was one mishap that changed the course of that night beyond expectation.

It was raining at 1:00 a.m. when Andrew and I left the church and walked over to the Mission Museum door. The plan was for Andrew to walk alone through the pitch-black labyrinth-like museum using (literally and metaphorically) what he had been given that night to navigate through the darkness. The intention was for me to open the door and say, "You have all that you need. I'll see you on the other side," and then close the door behind him as he entered the museum.

Yet despite all my planning, I reached out, grabbed the door handle, and pulled. "Shit! It's locked!" I jerked the handle several more times in disbelief.

I paused and looked over at Andrew drenched from the pouring rain. I took a deep breath and thought, *Maybe the backdoor is*

5

open and I can open the front door from the inside. I told Andrew, "Wait here," as I dashed over to the adjacent seven-foot wall and climbed over it. Praying as I ran, I stopped at the backdoor, wincing as I grabbed the handle and pulled. It swung wide open to my delight and I stepped inside exhaling in relief.

As my feet crossed the door threshold, time suddenly stood still. I could hear each creak of the door, as it slowly slammed shut behind me. I gasped! There I was in a pitch-black room. Total darkness. Like in the movie *Field of Dreams* (1989) where Shoeless Joe Jackson says, "No Ray, it was [for] you," my whole being knew in that moment that this, too, *was for me*. I stood there in the dark needing to make *my way* through the maze, just as I intended for my son. I began to weep, as I knew in my heart that *God showed up*—for me. In that failed moment, I experienced God with me in my efforts to be with my son.

In darkness, I slowly made my way to the front door and pushed on it—still locked. Through the door window, I motioned to Andrew to keep waiting. Returning to his side, I implemented a new plan—God's plan for us. Still raining, we walked over to the wall where our efforts to climb it were both strenuous and comical. That moment added dirt, rain, scrapes, and laughter to a tightly planned rite. It made it human and real, and for years afterward, we visited that wall on his birthday, touching it, sitting near it, while reflecting on the past year and the year to come.

After climbing the wall, we found our way to the backdoor of the museum. I took another deep breath and swung the door open as before. Holding it open, I instructed my son to navigate the same darkness from which I just emerged: "Find the front door, push on it, and if it doesn't open, return." He returned.

The rite ended with Andrew and me jumping naked into the Pacific Ocean at two in the morning. After the ordeal, we all went to the local Denny's. No words were needed. The looks on our faces displayed the awe over what had just happened. We knew that it was intimately who we are and at the same time much, much more.

Looking back, who I am as a Mexican American father emerged that night as I sought to initiate my son into a way of life, a way that I have come to now recognize in Hispanic spirituality. Ultimately, the snapshot provided by Andrew's initiation revealed a spirituality from the gut, born out of the struggle to be, that yearned to live *no longer just I, but we*—with, in, and through a God who walks with us.

That night also caused in me a shift in how I practice youth ministry, emphasizing the importance of symbolic, affective, bodily experiences and the power of interweaving narratives.

Later that year, I experienced a male rites-of-passage retreat in New Mexico. It was Richard Rohr's inaugural retreat of this kind, as he, too, was working on contemporary adaptations of traditional initiation rites. Attending with my dad, the retreat was powerful, involving symbols, rituals, teachings by Richard, and grief work.

In preparation for the retreat, we were asked to bring symbols that represent aspects of our lives, one of which was suffering. I wasn't sure what to bring, but I knew I was burdened by pain and grief, which often felt like an unbearable weight. To symbolize this weight, I bought a brick, drilled a hole in it, and slipped a rope through the hole to wear the brick around my neck. While packing for the retreat, I noticed brick dust getting on my clothes, so I decided to wrap the brick in duct tape.

On the day designated for grief, I wore the brick around my neck and soon discovered that the duct tape allowed me to cleanly write on it. Sitting alone in the mountainous terrain during times of reflection, I covered the brick with symbols and words, tracing one word, "DAD," over and over in large bold letters. Fortunately, in that moment, I overcame my reluctance to write the word in such a bold fashion, knowing that my dad was with me on this retreat.

As we sat for lunch that day, I saw my dad's eyes catch the word. His chewing slowed and taking a slow deep sigh, he glanced up at me and nodded ever so slightly.

Later that afternoon, we all experienced a ritual designed to symbolically split us open. I remember a man carving a line from my neck to my belly with iodine and feeling both torn apart and held by God at the same time. After this ritual action, the rite continued with an extended period of silence.

Maintaining silence, I found my dad, who was walking off toward a hillside. I walked up to him and, without any words, looked at him through streaming tears and handed him a knife. He took the knife and knew what to do.

He grabbed the rope and started cutting. The dull kitchen knife tore slowly through the strong braided rope as I jerked with each push and pull of my dad's arms. Finally, it was finished. Out of breath, my dad held the rope bound to the brick. We stood motionless for a second, then hugged for a meaningful second more. I turned and walked away dripping wet with a relief that only salvific longing can bring.

This powerful encounter added fuel to what began with my son's initiation. At its core, the seed that began to grow in my heart and mind was simple: our human longing (suffering) wants to find relief (transformation) in our encounters with each other and in our encounters with the Divine. They are narratives in search of each other.

❦

My work in youth ministry began in 1986 as a volunteer at St. Christopher in West Covina, California, and continued in 1988 as the director of youth ministry for *Alive Ministries,* a Catholic Charismatic young adult organization offering retreats, seminars, and workshops throughout the Archdiocese of Los Angeles. After graduating from Loyola Marymount University in 1992 with a bachelor of arts in theology, I was hired as youth minister at St. John the Evangelist in Encinitas (North County San Diego). It was there where I began to put into practice all that I gained from the transformative experiences with my son and my father.

In 1996, inspired by the nature of these experiences, a handful of leaders and I created *The Boat*—a gospel reenactment of Jesus and Peter walking on the water. To construct a full sensory experience, we threw several rowboats onto a stage, gathered seaweed, set up fans, created a soundtrack, wrote a simple script, and directed leaders to rock boats and read lines aloud—all to insert young people into the gospel story.

As part of the confirmation program, this constructed rite took place during our regular meeting times without the fore-knowledge of the confirmation candidates. My eleven-year-old son attended each session of the program that year, although he was years away from receiving the sacrament. At the start of this session, we blindfolded the candidates, led them to the stage, and placed them in a boat.

At the culmination of an experience filled with music, sound effects, live reading, and boat rocking, the candidates were sum-moned with these words: "Believe in the truth that Jesus stands before you, reaching out his hand beckoning you to step onto the water. When you hear your name called, step out of the boat in faith."

One by one, I called the name of each candidate and watched as each young person cautiously but eagerly stepped out of the boat while blindfolded. (Don't worry, leaders were standing by to ensure safety.)

When I got to my son, I stepped toward him and, without much forethought, called out his name. As the sound of his name traveled from my gut through my chest and windpipe and out of my mouth, I was struck by the pure visceral experience of the com-munion between us. Like the experience of his initiation (where we all felt that we were bodily and psycho-spiritually plugged into something bigger, grander, and Divine), *this moment caught me*, as I stood there, like Jesus with Peter, beckoning my son to literally step into mystery, into the unknown. I was equally moved to see my young eleven-year-old son joyfully spring out of the boat, in full trust after hearing my voice.

It was then that I knew that the gospel story could be made real for young people by inserting the familiar voice of love that had been in their lives all along—mom's loving voice, dad's loving voice. Inspired by that experience, the following year we invited (secretly) each parent to attend *The Boat*.

Quietly watching their teenage daughters and sons go through a storm experience while blindfolded, one by one, the parents stood up, stepped forward, and called out the name of their beloved child.

Overwhelmingly, the experience of that moment was evident on the faces of the parents and teenagers. They, too, were caught by the experience, and the parents later spoke of the power they felt as a parent and as the voice of Christ. They also spoke of their longing to have a deeply felt moment, like this, with their teenage sons and daughters—something they rarely experienced at this stage in their lives. The teenagers responded equally with excitement, joy, emotion, and giddiness over hearing their parents call out to them and over feeling their familiar arms guide them in the dark.

In the following years, we shifted the production of *The Boat* to include the parents (as secret observers) by adding a screen behind the boats showing stormy seas and lyrics to songs, as well as strobe lights during the storm, and inviting families to attend. We also involved our bilingual leaders in accompanying the Spanish-speaking parents throughout the process and included a Spanish translation of the song lyrics.

Gratefully, all of this was initiated not only by the salvific experience embodied by *The Boat*, but also by what *The Boat* taught us about bringing lives together within sacred space. Powerfully, *The Boat* carried a momentum toward love and others and continually expanded to include young people, parents, families, and other sacred narratives and symbols. All we really needed to do was trust this movement toward love by animating the salvific fullness that was there all along in the gospel story and in the loving relationships that surround our precious young people.

Reflecting on my time at St. John, I am grateful to have encountered such amazing young people and adult leaders, trying to do all we could to bring faith in Christ alive. I also wish I had expanded on the notion of interweaving narratives to include a deeper investment in culture and identity.

St. John is a multicultural parish with a vibrant Mexican community, and while the youth ministry program I directed involved a high percentage of youth and leaders of Mexican descent, I did not consider that I was "doing Hispanic ministry," especially since the parish offered strong programs in Spanish. I also did not consider myself a Hispanic pastoral leader, not because I was denying my Mexican identity, but because I did not connect my personal identity with the way in which I practiced ministry. On personal and ministerial levels, I failed to invest in the communion between who I am and how I practice ministry from within the most fundamental symbol of identity—culture.

In admitting this, I must also admit that my inability to speak Spanish carries a great deal of shame for me. It always has. Some might call me "Americanized," others "assimilated," and still others, "not Mexican." Whichever slant is uttered (or revealed in a glance), it always feels like a punch in the gut that tells me I don't belong. So, yes, in those days, I timidly professed my Mexicanness, not for lack of pride or ownership, but because I knew the statements that would follow; statements that diminished my authentic self: "But you don't speak Spanish." "You're not a real Mexican." "What happened?" "Why haven't you learned to speak Spanish?"

It wasn't until I entered the Doctor of Ministry program at Barry University in 2007 that I began to reflect deeply on the mixture of my culture, my identity, and pastoral ministry.

❧ ⁂ ❧

In 2006, I left St. John parish with the desire to continue my education and serve underresourced communities, which led me to work for the city of Santa Monica as team leader and case manager specialist for the Chronic Homeless program. As a housing-first model, my job took place in the streets, mostly in back alleys, encountering those facing severe challenges to their health, stability, and the sustainability of basic needs.

My experience in Santa Monica allowed me the privilege of accompanying and advocating for people overwhelmed by societal rejection and failed institutional systems. Within that context, my relationship with each person centered on their hardships exposed for all to see, which often included job loss, family loss, mental illness, addiction, tragedy, physical affliction, and misfortune.

In hearing the beautiful and heartbreaking life stories from people young and old, men and women, mothers and fathers, veterans and teenagers, I came to know each person not as a drug addict, outcast, or mentally ill person, but as Marie, George, Bill, Mary, Robin, Armando, and the many other beautiful names of the people I encountered. By removing the dehumanizing perceptions associated with homeless peoples, I became exposed to real beauty. I encountered people who possess an enormity of faith, joy, and gratitude. I witnessed a genuine sense of care for each other as a community, and I encountered powerful art created by amazing artists.

These encounters helped me realize that the homeless are no different from me, and me from them, each of us overcome by the shit of life, and yet longing to be seen, to be held, and to have a bed, a meal, and heat. With them and in them, I was moved to see our salvific communion through the experience of defeat, pain, and alienation. This strengthened my inclination to step into the suffering we all endure, knowing that beauty and life exist within the experiences of alienation we all share. Later, this empowered me to envision the practice of ministry from within the lives of the beautiful people living unprotected from societal care.

❧ ⸙ ☙

In mid-2007, I began serving the Dolores Mission Catholic Community in Boyle Heights, California, as youth minister and immersion coordinator. My perspective and focus had now widened to include both the influence of culture and identity, and the insistence that ministry must start with everyday life, which often includes painful and alienating experiences.

Dolores Mission Church is a Jesuit parish located in the Pico-Aliso area in Boyle Heights. Adjacent to East Los Angeles, it is a densely populated inner-city community consisting primarily of bilingual Mexican- and U.S.-born and/or raised young people.

While at Dolores Mission, I was also immersed in my doctoral studies at Barry University, a Dominican school in Miami

12

Shores, Florida. I had received my master's degree in theological studies from Loyola Marymount University in 2003 and was eager to further study pastoral theologies while emphasizing Hispanic ministry and theology. The doctoral program allowed me to live and work in Los Angeles, although it required flying to Miami twice a year, two weeks at a time, for intensive class work with other students from across the nation.

On my first trip to Miami, I realized I was the only one in the room who was not bilingual, which caused me great anxiety. Needing to *out* myself, I immediately shared my reality, including my shame. In each room, I sat and uttered out loud, "But I don't speak Spanish," and on each occasion, to my surprise, *I was welcomed*! I received words and gestures of overwhelming affirmation and acceptance. For the first time, I felt that I belonged somewhere as a monolingual, English-only Mexican American. Inspired by the sense of belonging and affirmation, I eagerly gave voice to my Mexican identity, which empowered me. As I shared my history, it was uplifting to hear others say, "Dude, you're so Mexican!"

Given my studies at Barry University and the insertion of my own identity into how I understand and practice ministry, Dolores Mission was a whirlwind of trying new things and further developing previous methods, all of which were the result of the confluence of four narrative pieces: the affirmation of my Mexican identity, the beauty of the Boyle Heights community, my experience in ministry, and the knowledge gained from studying Hispanic ministry and theology. At the intersection of these narratives was Dolores Mission, where I proudly self-identified as a Hispanic pastoral leader, serving inner-city Hispanic youth and doing Hispanic ministry.

It is fitting that a narrative approach took root and developed at Dolores Mission in service of a ministerial vision invested in the neighborhood and enacted in the streets. On my first day and as a powerful testament to this vision, the pastor at Dolores Mission, Scott Santarosa, SJ, walked me through the streets of the neighborhood, stopping at Pecan Park to introduce me to several youngsters. These same streets later became the focal point of my doctoral work designed to uncover the

narrative fragments and salvific themes in *"cariño*-fighting,"
which is discussed in chapter 2.

By stepping into their space, the challenges facing the youth
of this community became apparent and moved us deeper into
their narratives, into the areas that affect them most, such as education, employment, immigration, violence, gang life, healthcare,
street life, and identity. The fullness of these experiences at Dolores
Mission is reflected in the stories throughout this book, and I am
genuinely grateful for the impact this experience bestowed on my
life, especially in exposing my unique Mexican nature.

At Dolores Mission, my *Latinamente* came alive through the
life of the Boyle Heights community. I felt it through the warm
embraces of the people; the genuine hospitality; the abundant
opportunities to celebrate, laugh, and eat; and in the beautiful
spirituality manifested in the cultural and religious life of the
community.

These experiences inspired deeper reflection on my way-of-
being, as part of my personal quest to fully uncover the Mexican
cultural and religious narratives alive in my life. Until then, I had
always struggled to find my Mexican identity through traditional
cultural expressions, which I did not recognize in my life, especially given the assimilated nature of my upbringing. Yet the life of
this community inspired me to look deeper into *who I am* and *how
I am*, exposing the ways in which my Mexican American identity
comes alive. Consequently, I found my unique identity within the
totality of my life.

I found my identity in my longing for encounters and experiences of community, of the Divine, and of mystery. And I found
it in the need for these experiences to be somatic, affective, symbolic, sensory, communal, and transformative.

I found my identity in the animation of my son's initiation rite, in the brick experience with my Dad, and in the ritual-
symbolic, performance-driven activities produced in my work
with young people.

I found my identity in each step taken, walking in street processions and protest marches.

I found my identity in my desire for liturgies that intimately connect to and transform daily life.

I found my identity in my emotional reaction on hearing the mariachi song, *Malagueña*.

I found my identity in my attraction to movies, symbols, art, performance, music, food, and celebration.

I found it in my belief in miracles, my connection to my ancestors, in the wearing of my religious bracelet, and in the medallions that serve as powerful reminders of my union with loved ones.

I found my identity in my deeply felt connection to Ash Wednesday and Good Friday, and in my home altar where my grandmother's statue of *La Virgen* rests.

Of course, such narrative expressions are not exclusive to a Mexican way-of-being, but they are necessarily revealed through *my history of being*—connected to my family, my ancestors, my religion, and my Mexican blood.

Looking back at my time at Dolores Mission, I am grateful to this small community for animating the salvific fullness that was in my life all along, empowering me to fully participate in a much larger narrative.

❧ ⬥ ☙

Unfortunately, after nearly two years, my time at Dolores Mission finished, resulting from the economic crash of 2008.

In 2011, I was contracted by the Diocese of Fresno to coordinate a leadership-based bilingual Hispanic Ministry Convocation. The convocation utilized a see-judge-act methodology, with emphasis on giving voice to the context, needs, and hopes of leaders in Hispanic ministry throughout the diocese. In preparing for the convocation, we were concerned that many pastoral leaders might not attend given that Hispanic ministry is widely viewed in terms of language, as ministry in Spanish. This meant that, although the high Hispanic population in the Central Valley suggested that most pastoral leaders were serving Hispanics in their communities, many did not consider their ministry as Hispanic ministry (much like my earlier experience), especially if offered in

English (or if everyone participating spoke English), and, if pastoral leaders themselves were not Hispanic.

Consequently, we invested in communicating the broad identity and language spectrum that defines Hispanic ministry, which, significantly, includes ministry with first-generation immigrants who often only speak Spanish, but also includes the 1.5-, second-, and third-generation Hispanics who are often bilingual/bicultural or limited in Spanish proficiency. We also attempted to expand the spectrum related to pastoral leaders serving Hispanic communities, which importantly includes leaders who are Hispanic, but also includes many other leaders who are not Hispanic. This spectrum likewise includes leaders (Hispanic and non-Hispanic) who do not speak Spanish. Promoting this broad identity-language spectrum, our efforts proved fruitful with over six hundred pastoral leaders attending the three-day event.

Overall, many pastoral leaders spoke about the spirit of belonging and the felt connectivity they experienced by sitting side by side and hearing each other's struggles and dreams in different languages. This energy, inspiration, and joy encouraged us to continue to promote the expanded nature of Hispanic ministry in the years following the convocation.

Within this spirit, the ongoing conversation concerning the range of Hispanic identities and Hispanic ministry leaders is crucial for us to serve the growing number of Hispanic youth in the United States today properly, and for Hispanic ministry—its function and meaning—to be a contributing force in these efforts.

❧ ⸪ ❧

That same year, I began my tenure as the director of Santa Teresita Youth Conference Center (STYCC), a 146-bed youth retreat facility operated by the Diocese of Fresno, which stretches geographically from Bakersfield to Yosemite, serving a predominantly Hispanic population, many of whom live in impoverished rural and inner-city communities.

When I arrived at STYCC, construction of the retreat facility had just begun, and, as the founding director, I was responsible for hiring staff and developing policies, budgets, programs, and long-term plans. Drawing from the momentum of the Hispanic Ministry Convocation, I hit the road to visit pastoral leaders and parish communities in order to hear their stories and assess needs.

As I grew in my understanding of their economic struggles, it became evident that over 90 percent of the pastoral leaders serving youth were volunteers running programs without resources, formation, time, or financial support. The ministerial challenges related to these circumstances prompted me to put aside our original ideas and instead prioritize leadership development. It seemed too disjointed to try and convince pastoral leaders to use our facilities when many did not have the opportunity to develop leaders and build a retreat team. As a result, we developed and offered a series of leadership offerings that included working with parish teams to develop retreats, some of which did not take place at STYCC due to geographic and financial challenges.

Another one of these offerings included the *How to Build a Retreat–Retreat.* Significantly, this retreat gave us the opportunity to further invest in a narrative approach, which had already proved so fruitful. Related to this approach, this retreat was designed to name and model retreat strategies like the following: identifying the movements in a retreat (from *a* to *b*, from broken to forgiven); developing naming activities to give voice to pains/struggles/joys; and creating experiential moments using powerful biblical stories—all for interweaving narratives—to see their stories in our stories (and vice versa), and to inspire healing and transformation.

Energized by these experiences and by the response from leaders, we moved deeper into this narrative approach by developing what I had initiated at Dolores Mission—*The Identity Project,* which engages young Hispanic leaders over a lengthy period to facilitate the narration of *who they are* through dialogue and artistic performance. As an artistic-driven endeavor, *The Identity Project* empowers the creative nature of young people to talk about, create, design, write, rehearse, and perform pieces of their lives.

We traveled to underresourced parishes throughout the diocese to meet with young Hispanics and talk about their lives using four identity-related questions:

Who are you?

Where do you come from?

What are your dreams?

Who is your God?

Through a series of dialogue sessions, we got to know these amazing young people and hear their stories. In sitting together, we learned about who they are. For example, we learned that they had rich stories of how their parents met in Mexico. We heard tragic, joyful, and funny stories about their families crossing the border. We learned that the border, shoes, food, family, and Christmas were strong symbols connecting them to their cultural and faith identities. From adults we learned that some of their parents grew up on corn tortillas while others grew up on flour, depending on the region in which they lived, and that some were considered a "mixed marriage" because mom was flour and dad was corn.

We also learned that "Who is your God?" was the most challenging question to answer, but that their experiences and expressions of God were rooted in family, so we kept going back to the stories of "Where did you come from?" and "Who are you?" to talk about God. We learned that prayer was deeply important to them, and their most common name for God is "God." We learned that they struggle with their cultural identity. We learned from them that finding a significant other is challenging and often leaves them feeling lonely. We learned that most dreamed of family and careers dedicated to helping others: teachers, social workers, doctors, psychiatrists, and the like. We learned that they highly value education but are faced with many challenges to obtain access. And we learned that they love to laugh and be together.

Overall, *The Identity Project* affirmed our belief in the capacity of young people to express their deepest thoughts and aspirations, as well as in their ability to create something born from their lives connected to the lives of their peers. By giving young people opportunity, resources, and support, we witnessed their salvific essence come alive through their self-expressions, creative spirit, and intimate communion with each other. Through this endeavor, we became the ones transformed by their offerings to

God, their prayers reflected in their words and in their art. They, in turn, became the ones giving us hope and inspiring us to continue to build retreats and offerings based on who they are and who they long to be.

❦ ⋖⋗ ❦

Meanwhile, during that period in my life, a significant non-STYCC-related event occurred that demonstrated God's continued presence in my life despite all my flaws and misgivings.

As a final narrative, God once again revealed God's self by bringing Patty into my life, and we married on August 13, 2011. Patty Jimenez was born in Ensenada, Mexico, and migrated to the United States as a child. By age five, she learned to speak English and self-identifies as a bilingual/bicultural 1.5-generation Mexican. I met Patty at Barry University, where she, too, was studying to earn her doctorate in ministry. We both graduated in 2014.

Our wedding was beautifully planned, mostly by Patty, and included many Mexican traditions. The wedding mass included mariachis, *padrinos* and *madrinas*, a rosary used as a unity lace (*el lazo*), the presentation of coins (*las arras*), and a prayer and gift to Our Lady of Guadalupe (*ofrenda*). I was especially moved as we chanted a litany calling for our ancestors to be with us.

As the time for our vows drew near, I nervously stood in front of Patty wearing my white linen guayabera shirt. Holding her hands, I looked into her eyes and then glanced over to Fr. Jorge Presmanes, our beloved professor from Barry. He nodded and said, "Repeat after me." To Patty's surprise, and with the help of Fr. Jorge, I proceeded to recite my wedding vows—*in Spanish*.

It was a spontaneous action, having presented the idea to Fr. Jorge the day before. It made perfect sense to express my communion with her in Spanish. I worked on the pronunciation that night but was relieved by Fr. Jorge's idea. I repeated the traditional vows, spoken first by him, with the words flowing from my mouth flawlessly. At least that's what I remember.

With the mariachi band playing as we recessed out of the chapel, I felt a deep communion with my new wife, expressed

19

through the symbols, sounds, music, and language of our culture and our faith. It was truly salvific.

These are the precious narratives of my life, graced with the painful and beautiful struggle to be washed over by a loving God. In human terms, they illustrate my search to find relief and transformation in the arms of loved ones and God. Essentially, this book is a tribute to this grand salvific reality alive in all of us.

2

Proposing a Narrative Approach to Ministry with Young People

Why a Narrative Approach?

*W*hen we hear the word *narrative*, we think *story*, with a beginning, middle, and end, usually communicated through written, oral, and artistic mediums. This understanding of story provides the basis for a narrative approach to ministry designed to draw attention to the pieces, parts, and dimensions of the stories alive in each person. This approach also draws attention to the depth and multitude of narratives that, when pieced together, make up larger narratives, connecting each person to a family, culture, generation, community, and the ongoing Christian narrative.

Our narratives are also different from story since they do not necessarily appear with clear beginnings and triumphant endings, but are incomplete, fragmented, and ongoing. Nor are they limited to written, oral, or artistic forms since the pieces and fragments of a person's life are sometimes left private, hidden, disconnected, and unconscious. Such fragmented narratives and the wholeness they seek are what have driven the development of this narrative approach.

One of the greatest gifts I have received in my life is the opportunity to work with a psychotherapist, focusing on the disconnected parts of me that long to be voiced, healed, and integrated into my entire being—parts of me that involve shame, fear, creativity, anger, and a longing to be worthy and belong. Operating from a Jungian perspective, much of our work together involves unearthing the parts of me that are not clearly known to my conscious mind but show up in my dreams, in my bodily pain and mental anguish, in my yearnings and hopes, and in my core feelings and life experiences.

Like all people, I possess layers of narrative pieces, connected and disconnected, voiced and hidden, each longing to belong and be linked to other narrative pieces, hoping to experience the beauty and fullness of who I am—as someone connected to larger narratives involving family, culture, community, and faith life. As this integration happens, my narrative pieces transform into experiences that bring me immense joy and salvific meaning and enliven my God-given relational essence. This example represents what I mean by narrative within a life-giving approach.

The previous chapter is also a testament to the development of this narrative approach that I stumbled over and pieced together as I persisted in nurturing my personal life and the lives of the many young people I have encountered. Through the years, the salvific essence in our collective lives grew louder and more recognizable to me and compelled me not only to seek greater understanding of it, but also to consider perspectives and strategies that may be useful to how we practice ministry—if we could somehow plug into and support the salvific nature we already possess. (In the next chapter, we expand on the salvific essence alive in each person, as it relates to a narrative approach.)

At St. John, I noticed early on that experiences like *The Boat* generated opportunities for young people to give voice to their fragmented selves, as I witnessed the transformational glimpses that occurred as they uttered (writing, speaking, or drawing) their pains in relational space. Naturally, this led us to consider ways to carry these fragments toward healing and wholeness, often involving ongoing presence, family, communal prayer and resources, and local professionals.

Nevertheless, the challenge of how to uncover and tend to the hidden or unarticulated parts of young people's lives remained, especially since those parts were neither obvious nor discussed. I took this curiosity with me to Dolores Mission, where ministry often took place in the streets, beyond liturgical and church space. It was there that I caught glimpses of interactions, of bodily expressions, of identity markers, which, again, made me wonder about the meaning and connectivity behind such expressions.

As a primary example, I observed a high frequency of fighting between friends, not only among teenage boys, but also among girls. In 2009, my interest in this act grew when I asked some teenagers what this act meant to them. A tough-as-nails fifteen-year-old girl responded, "We fight out of *cariño*," which means, we fight out of affection and caring. Inspired by her words, I came to call this type of fighting, *cariño*-fighting.[1]

In observing this act in the streets, in the park, in front yards, and even on the parish grounds, my desire to understand this act grew as I heard over and over that it somehow symbolized relationality, fun, identity, aggression, and the bodily longing to feel true kinship. Although covered in a shroud of violence, I explored the act so that I could see and give voice to the narrative fragments and surrounding life circumstances connected to it.

Implementing the work that I had initiated years ago at St. John and drawing from a wealth of influential works,[2] I developed a functioning narrative approach to ministry to examine, in part, such acts as *cariño*-fighting.[3]

By opening up *cariño*-fighting using a narrative methodology, I discovered a complex act that embodies a confluence of narrative layers including street life, bodily identity, the prevalence of gang violence, public daily life, poverty, the code of respect and shame, play, the popular religiosity of the community, and the longing to experience a felt kinship with friends who together live outside the care of the community.[4] In uncovering these layers, salvific themes emerged that surprisingly linked to the religiosity of the neighborhood, creating pathways to understand the salvific longing of these youth within the life of the faith community.[5]

Following this work, I continued to develop and clarify a narrative approach for ministry. The following story best captures its essence and fruitfulness, and can be viewed in the context of the surrounding narratives uncovered in *cariño*-fighting.

This story about Dolores Mission presents Boyle Heights's youth who live in a distinct context that may differ from other socioeconomic realities affecting Hispanic young people throughout the United States. Recognizing each distinct context is important because the salvific narratives we wish to uncover emerge out of these everyday landscapes. Conversely, given that distinctions in settings matter, this story also draws attention to the salvific nature and transformative process alive in the youth of Boyle Heights and alive in all the young people we serve. By sharing stories from a specific location, both the uniqueness and sameness come alive and expose us to a distinct world, yes, but one to which we are all connected in a deeply human and salvific way. Thus, in capturing the essence of a narrative approach, the following story reveals both the beauty of these specific young people and the transformative process in which we all participate.

The Haunted House Story

Dolores Mission Catholic parish has long been a popular immersion destination for Catholic universities, especially because of the parish ties to Greg Boyle, SJ, who founded Homeboy Industries at Dolores Mission, and because of the realities of the community (a beautiful sense of faith, justice, and hope within the context of poverty and violence). As the immersion coordinator, I organized the overall structure and activities of immersion stays, which would typically last from three to seven days. I placed students in neighborhood homes and coordinated educational forums and interactions with the Dolores Mission School students, the men at the on-site homeless shelter, and visits to Homeboy Industries, Homegirl Café, and Homeboy Silkscreen.

Soon after my initial immersion experiences with universities, I sought ways to shift the overall spirit of the program from students serving the marginalized to young adults encountering and walking with the people of the community. At the same time, as youth minister, I was also looking for ways for the neighborhood youth to give voice to their lives and tell their stories.

In response to both, I asked some of the local young people, who self-identified as *street* and called themselves the *Youngsters*, to hang out with college students and just talk. It was an unusual request since most had never been asked to interact with others outside the neighborhood at such a personal level. I, too, didn't know what to expect since the only directive was to talk, which meant the language would be spicy and the topics would get real. Neither was a concern for me; in fact, that was my hope, so I made sure not to add restrictions that might inhibit genuine interaction.

For my part, all I really did was invite the *Youngsters*, buy pizza, and set up chairs. Each event, however, was truly amazing. Questions about everything went back and forth. The interactions were lively and there was much laughter and a wide range of topics. Then there were these moments when it got deep: a twenty-year-old sharing stories about how his best friend was shot at the park and died in his arms; a fourteen-year-old talking about his brother in jail; a seventeen-year-old sharing that he was undocumented, and then one of the students admitting she too was also undocumented; a fifteen-year-old telling us about her dream to go to Brown University and play softball; others talking about wanting to become a fireman, a dance choreographer, and so forth. Underneath it all, what I observed was that maybe for the first time in their lives, someone was truly interested in them, in their lives, with value and respect, wanting to hear their stories.

As each one spoke, I could see an empowerment, a *concientización*, an internal raising of self-awareness, emerge around their own value, agency, and strength made real by giving voice to their lives in relational space.

During one of these gatherings, one of the older *Youngsters* shared his experience of a haunted house in his old neighborhood that he would frequent as a kid. The others talked about how they couldn't have something like that today because the neighborhood was too hot—it was too dangerous. The idea, however, must have captured their imagination because the next day they came to me with enthusiasm. They wanted to create a haunted house in the bungalow (the youth-designated portable building in the church parking lot).

I was also excited about the idea, so I quickly presented it to our *equipo*, our pastoral team. I could see the worry on many of their faces and some even objected due to potential violence in the neighborhood. However, the *equipo* also saw the value in supporting our youth and rallied around the project providing resources and community buy-in. Even the men in the parish homeless shelter were part of this event, wearing bright yellow security T-shirts made and donated by Homeboy Silkscreen.

We spent weeks converting the bungalow into a scary and thrilling haunted house experience. Each young person brought something to contribute: materials, paint, fake blood, scary figures, masks, lights, candy, and food. Together they worked hard and displayed their creative ideas, as they completed a multistage maze suitable for all ages.

Overall, the night was amazing, with over 150 neighborhood kids attending the haunted house. As an added surprise, in the middle of the event, the *Youngsters* told me they needed to temporarily shut down the haunted house to watch their friend (also a *Youngster*) perform his dance routine at the local park next door. I was naturally caught off guard and resisted at first, but their commitment to one of their own was unwavering.

So, we shut down the haunted house for about half an hour and walked over to the park to cheer him on. Nobody got upset, the kids waited in line for it to reopen, and we came back and continued without missing a beat. It was a rare moment of true kinship. It was also a great teaching moment, showing *me* that there is nothing more valuable than our engagement with those we love.

In all, voiced in the context of the struggles of the neighborhood and the challenges of their lives, the broken beauty of *their stories* took center stage. Through them, we were captivated and drawn into their *vida cotidiano* (everyday life), which opened our eyes to see the narrative pieces connected to their lives, such as neighborhood violence, hope, laughter, immigration, incarceration, poverty, education, play, career, kinship, and community. In turn, the spaces we created generated a creative confidence for them to give voice to their longing for a new narrative to happen, a narrative where the neighborhood is safe and kids-could-be-kids and have fun protected and surrounded by the people of the community.

This dynamic between their lives and our lives underscores two important dimensions related to narrative and ministry. First, the haunted house story uncovers, for us, the salvific nature of narrative, that is, the movement outward from giving voice in shared space to deeper community involvement. While not every narrative occasion leads to big community events, pastoral leaders must stay attuned to the reality that the narrative pieces of their lives always want to be more, want to be connected, healed, and transformed both personally and communally, which leads us to the second dimension: the role of pastoral leaders.

In this approach, pastoral leaders must recognize and assist the salvific movement of narrative. Often, this means that our function is to set up chairs. In other words, pastoral leaders are called to intentionally create space for youth simply to be and share. Equally important, we are also called to be present in those moments, to be empathically available to have our eyes opened by them. That way, the felt connection we experience motivates our commitment to the ongoing accompaniment of the narrative fragments that appear in those moments.

Imagine if the haunted house idea had stalled or was denied. It would have felt like yet another rejection to the *Youngsters*, and the weeks we spent together planning, arguing, and creating would never have happened. Furthermore, I wonder if everything after the haunted house would have ever taken place. The group went on to organize clean-up days, a magic mountain trip, and movie nights; to attend social justice events; to start a leadership group; and, for some, to participate in the confirmation program. We even proposed and attended a reverse immersion planned by Loyola Marymount University students, taking about fifteen youth to LMU for a day.

All of this happened because they were empowered, as their pains and desires were revealed through narrative occasions, but also because we pastoral leaders were committed to the ongoing accompaniment of the narrative fragments revealed by these precious youth. From this perspective, we can say that in a narrative approach, pastoral leaders are called to step into a narrative process that carries its own momentum *and* assist this process by actively engaging in the movement of narratives toward relational wholeness. While there are many life-affirming aspects embodied in this haunted house narrative, overall, it illustrates the innate momentum and salvific capacity embodied in the acts of giving voice and nurturing salvific narratives.

Certainly, the haunted house story helps us see the transformative power intended in a narrative approach. Yet, while it is important to see it in action, we also need to understand it in practical/useful terms in such a way that we can apply this approach to the ways in which we do ministry. While part 3 of this book specifically articulates the practical function and strategies of this approach, let's now examine briefly an outline of the approach in three movements, including a list of corresponding strategies. This outline introduces the complete approach—in its entirety and its parts—built upon the premise that the primary function of ministry is to uncover and nurture the salvific narratives in the lives of the people of our communities.

An Outline for a Narrative Approach to Ministry with Youth

SEE AND GIVE VOICE TO THE EVERYDAY LIVES OF YOUNG PEOPLE

The process begins with the work of *seeing*, as an adapted form of the see-judge-act methodology.[6] This involves stepping into the daily lives of young people, shifting the location where ministry happens, and *giving voice* to the narrative pieces evident in the totality of their lives. Importantly, providing space, opportunity, and resources for these narratives to be voiced by the youth themselves (in the expressive forms they choose) is fundamental. By giving voice to their narrative pieces, they can express a deeper sense of who they are as persons who long to experience love and salvation; who long to be forgiven, healed, and nurtured; who feel broken and alone; and who seek purpose and meaning in their daily existence. Through this work of seeing and giving voice, we begin the process of uncovering and naming these salvific narratives alive in their lives.

> *Strategy 1*: Trust the Salvific Essence Alive in Young People
>
> *Strategy 2*: See How Young People are Connected and Disconnected
>
> *Strategy 3*: Can We Just Stop Talking?
>
> *Strategy 4*: Give Voice Always and Everywhere
>
> *Strategy 5*: Convert Statements into Questions
>
> *Strategy 6*: Name the Salvific Themes We See

BRINGING NARRATIVES TOGETHER BY BRINGING LIVES TOGETHER

Having invested in seeing and giving voice to the narratives that reveal who they are, we now nurture the work of *bringing narratives together by bringing lives together*. This is where the community brings forth people to walk with young people toward healing and fullness of life. Here, we are called to respond to the narrative fragments we see and hear, emphasizing our care for the painful, hidden, and unspoken aspects in the lives of young people. Often, this involves a village of relationships including professionals and local services that can address specific needs like those related to mental illness, addiction, education, immigration, employment, and healthcare.

Here, too, is where we raise awareness and seek restoration of the failed social structures, institutional systems, and societal attitudes that perpetuate discrimination, harm, and the exclusion of young people, especially young people of color.

In bringing lives together, we are also called to animate the life-giving relationships in families, neighborhoods, and the faith community. Specifically, this involves facilitating dialogue and interaction between young people and older generations to connect and explore the common and distinct narratives that appear as sources of tension but also serve to join generations together.

> *Strategy 7*: Participate in Movement and Continue the Narrative
>
> *Strategy 8*: Foreground the Hidden Narratives
>
> *Strategy 9*: Dialogue between Generations

Transforming Narratives and the Animation of Sacred Space

Here, we continue to enter the salvific essence of young people by intentionally creating opportunities and sacred spaces for them to experience the transformational power that comes from interweaving their daily life narratives with biblical narratives and the ongoing Christian narrative, including the beautiful popular religiosity evident in Hispanic culture.

In accompanying the communion between the lives of young people, God, and the faith community, our role mirrors that of Eli, as one who points to and inspires a response much like the salvific response of Samuel to the LORD, "Speak, for your servant is listening" (1 Sam 3:10). As young people utter these words in voice, action, and expression, they are empowered to imagine new narratives for themselves and for the community. These transformative narratives bring alive the fullness of their salvific nature as they step further into faith and communal life as leaders tending to the communal need for wholeness, healing, justice, and happiness.

> *Strategy 10*: Continue the Narratives in Hispanic Catholic Popular Religiosity
>
> *Strategy 11*: Create Ritual Experiences
>
> *Strategy 12*: Inspire Transformative Responses Using Scripture

Overall, this brief outline articulates a process that remains committed to God alive in young people and in the communities that surround them. As we proceed into the specific living narratives of

Hispanic young people (part 2) and encounter each strategy (part 3), the life of this approach will continue to inspire our imagination and enlighten the ways in which we serve the young people of our communities.

In conclusion, I am reminded of the words of Elizabeth Johnson shared to me by systematic theologian Gloria Schaab, SSJ. In short, she advised, "Our work must not be about everything but is most fruitful when we take a long deep slice into one thing." The long deep slice, here, centers on the narrative approach that is built upon what God has created in us. Ultimately, what makes narratives salvific is what makes human beings salvific, making the notion of salvation the central life-giving paradigm on which we enact ministry. Let us now examine this paradigm more deeply.

3

The Salvific Nature of Being Human

*I*n 1998, as part of the leadership team at St. John, we constructed an experiential activity centered on two major themes, birth and death. Designed for confirmation candidates, the experience concluded with a prayer using candles to remember loved ones who had passed away. Gathered in a room of thirty teenagers, I noticed a few girls who were grieving during the prayer. They were huddled together sobbing; there were no words, but they were demonstrably in pain.

In that moment, they expressed something about themselves, a narrative piece that said they were suffering. Obviously, the experiential prayer did not create their pain. It had been present within them for some time. However, the prayer did create the space for them to express their pain, and for me to step into this painful part of their lives.

Soon after the prayer concluded, I walked over to the girls and awkwardly stood by them in silence. One of them, Katy, looked at me, and I smiled empathetically and said, "I'm sorry for your loss. Do you want to talk about it?" Katy, Jessie, and Liz pulled me aside, and we sat down to talk. They shared with me that their best friend had committed suicide almost a year ago. Understandably, they were still devastated and mourning his death. They tearfully spoke about their friend and shared their pain over the tragic incident. They also mentioned that the anniversary was approaching.

Before they departed, I asked if they wanted to keep talking about it, but with someone who could better accompany their grief. They all said yes. I contacted the parents of each to talk about the experience, and each shared that their daughter had been struggling all year. We arranged for the girls to come together later that week with a therapist who specialized in grief.

Hoping to create a safe, sacred space that didn't overlap with the busyness of their day, the session happened at 10:00 p.m. inside the church. Unlike a typical therapy session, the gathering included scripture readings and symbols of their friend, and took place in the space between the altar and the giant crucifix hanging on the wall. That space seemed fitting, since it smelled and felt like sacred space, symbolizing the sacred communion between life, death, and resurrection. For my part, again, all I did was set up the chairs.

After the scripture readings, I sat in the back of the church with the parents, while the girls and the therapist talked. Afterward, we all spoke for a little while and the girls appeared comforted, relieved, and grateful. Katy expressed her desire for her classmates also to share in a special gathering, telling us that this experience was helpful, and she wanted something for her friends who were also in pain. Because the anniversary was approaching, I suggested a memorial Mass, which the parish could help arrange.

They all lit up at the idea and eagerly committed to preparing for the Mass. Each worked hard at creating memorial cards, advertising, and preparing the liturgy. It was as if the work gave them the opportunity to move, sweat, grieve, create, and participate in the life and memory of their companion.

The church was filled with high school students, many of whom were not Catholic, and the girls and others gave testimony to the life of their friend while offering comforting words to their classmates. During the entire Mass, I remember feeling overwhelmed by the genuine desire of the students to share, hug, talk, sing, cry, listen, laugh, and pray. In this communal space, they expressed true care and love for one another, in grief and in loving memory of their beloved friend.

For us the story ends here, but for the girls, understandably their grieving continued, which required the ongoing accompaniment of family and community.

At its heart, this story serves to introduce the salvific essence alive in young people by illustrating its central theme: *movement*. Indeed, we have already alluded to this core element, having emphasized the movement toward each other, God, and self, as central to our salvific nature.

There's something about that movement that God has made in us, and I am caught every time I see it or am a part of it. Yes, it is connected to God alive in Christ, but it is also intimately ours, in our bones and breath, stuck at times and fearful at other times. Still, we move toward each other; upon hearing the weeping of the three girls, we moved toward them.

Filled with meaningful human interactions, the story of the girls contains the fundamental image of this movement, of the relationship between opposites revealed by a significant symbolic image—the crucifix. The setting of the story begins during a symbolic-ritual experience based on the paschal mystery we recite in every Mass: Christ has died, Christ is risen, Christ will come again. We see this pattern (birth, death, and new life) throughout nature and, in constructing the ritual, we animated this pattern, revealing it as a fundamental pattern of our lives.

The crucifix appears again in the story as the setting shifts to the space between the altar and the crucifix, between death and resurrection, grief and new life. The girls and the therapist grieving together in this space calls our attention to the power of the crucifix in our lives, prompting images of clutching a crucifix in our hands or gazing upon it in our times of great pain. In these moments, we surrender to the relationship the crucifix signifies—the relationship between the cross and resurrection, to the in-between space where God holds onto both through Christ's outstretched arms, revealing God's nearness, leading to our resurrection and new life. In this, we hear the words of the mystic Meister Eckhart: "Thus, the darkness glorifies God, and the light shines in it, not so much as opposites placed next to each other, but rather as opposites placed within each other."[1]

By bringing the crucifix—in symbol, ritual, and action—into the foreground, we see the paschal mystery experienced by the three girls more deeply by recognizing the communion they experienced between the cross and resurrection, between brokenness and human longing for healing, and between death and new life.

Through the salvific layers alive in this story, we can consider their implication for pastoral leaders. Our intent, here, is not to provide an all-encompassing summation of salvation, but rather to conclude, on a basic level, that human beings possess a salvific nature created by God. Furthermore, initiated by God, we possess the capacity to participate in salvation since *it is what God has made in us and it is how God is salvific with us*. In fact, that is what makes us salvific beings and that is why all narratives in our lives are salvific; for all the pieces of our lives happen within the gaze of God's grace, mercy, and love.

Second, believing that to be true, we must consider how our salvific nature is manifested in our daily lives. If we can identify this manifestation, even imperfectly and incompletely, then we can dare to consider how the faith community and pastoral leaders might function as a communal body invested in supporting and nurturing the salvific lives of our young people.

To enter more deeply into this reflection on salvation, we need to look no further than the beginning of Sacred Scripture. Our long deep slice into salvation leads us to examine the Creation narratives in Genesis.

What God Has Created in Us

Birthed as God's image, as *imago Dei*, human life begins as a unique relationship, a shared participation between God and humanity: "So God created humankind in his image, / in the image of God he created them; / male and female he created them" (Gen 1:27).

In this Genesis narrative, humanity is created in the image of a God that Christianity defines as an ontological relationship, as Trinity. Catherine LaCugna, in *God for Us: The Trinity and Christian Life*, presents a fascinating anthological excavation of doctrinal and theological assessments of the Trinity beginning with the Cappadocians in the fourth century CE to the present time.[2] Overall, her conclusion is expressed in her title: *God for Us*.

Through her rich analysis, LaCugna asserts that the God known to humanity is the God that exists, wherein human life intimately shares in *the one life of the triune God*: "The life of God is not something that belongs to God alone. Trinitarian life is also our life. As soon as we free ourselves from thinking that there are two levels to the Trinity, one *ad intra*, the other *ad extra*, then we see that there is one life of the triune God, a life in which we graciously have been included as partners."[3]

Created in God's image, we are created to be in-relationship, wherein God's relationality gives life to the relationality of all creation: "Divine relationality becomes the paradigm for every type of relationality in creation."[4] LaCugna continues: "The doctrine of the Trinity is not ultimately a teaching about 'God' but a teaching about *God's life with us and our life with each other*. It is a life of communion and indwelling, God in us, we in God, all of us in each other."[5]

LaCugna provides a substantive theological basis for understanding the inherent human-Divine interrelatedness that cradles and gives life to what it means to be created in the image of a triune God. To continue further into the depth of this relational dynamic, especially as it relates to the intimate nature of our salvific life, we turn again to the beginning, to the creation of humanity in the second Genesis story of Creation and the fall.

Bones of My Bones, Flesh of My Flesh

In the second Creation story, God physically and intimately molds and shapes the first human person. In paschal fashion, God takes, breaks down, builds up, and breathes, as God emanates physical love and communion. Noted theologian Dietrich Bonhoeffer recognizes in this moment "the bodily nearness of the Creator to the creature [revealing God's] concern, his thought for me, his design for me, his nearness to me."[6] For Hebrew scripture scholar, Claus Westermann, this powerful moment reveals that "to exist as a human being then is to exist in undivided unity."[7]

Following this creative act, God places the human among the two trees in the garden, commands the human not to eat the fruit of one of them, then, as described by Westermann, "the tension begins: the man is not yet the creature that God planned; there is something that is still 'not good,' namely that the man is alone, v. 18a."[8] Like a profound interlude, God announces, "It is not good that the man should be alone" (Gen 2:18).[9]

The significance of this sharp pronouncement resides not only within the statement itself, but also where it happens in the story. It happens within the context of creation, highlighting two seemingly contrasting realities contributing to what it means to be human. To be alone is *not good*, yet, as God's creation, humanity is *very good*: "God saw everything that he had made, and indeed, it was very good" (Gen 1:31). Feminist scripture scholar Phyllis Trible believes that "the divine evaluation 'it is not good for the earth creature to be alone' contrasts wholeness with isolation."[10]

As the story continues, in response to the experience of *aloneness*,[11] God acknowledges that, without human-to-human communion, humanity is incomplete. Consequently, God acts to bring to life and make real the relational identity of humanity. Phyllis Trible notes, "According to Yahweh God, what the earth creature needs is a companion, one who is neither subordinate nor superior; one who alleviates isolation through identity."[12]

The creation of the woman, as the completion of humanity, is monumental to the narrative (see Gen 2:21–23). In the creation of this new relational reality, the man cries out joyfully and weeps. "This at last is bone of my bones and flesh of my flesh" (Gen 2:23). For Trible, "these words speak unity, solidarity, mutuality, and equality."[13] This passage, for Westermann, announces the completion of humanity as *one flesh*, which is, "spiritual unity, the most complete personal community."[14]

Thus, from the creation of the first human, to the announcement that *to be alone is not good*, to the creation of human-to-human relationality, the Genesis Creation narrative reveals that we are built to be in-relationship. We are created out of love and for love. We are beings whose inherent relational identity is awakened through the simple physical human connection with others. *To-be-in-relationship* is therefore the primary purpose and function of what it means to be a person. Robert Goizueta makes this very point: "The ultimate goal of all human action is nothing other than the active participation in relationships and the enjoyment of those relationships, wherein the particularity of each person can be affirmed and allowed to flower."[15]

It Is Not Good to Be Alone

Unfortunately, our innate relationality that defines what it means to be human exists in tension with the universal human experience of isolation and alienation. We can also conclude that this pervasive human experience is as innate to who we are as is our relationality. To illustrate, we return to the story's announcement, "It is not good that the man should be alone" (Gen 2:18). In these words, we hear, for the first time in Scripture, the naming of a human pathos, of human suffering—to be alone—voiced by God in the context of creation. Here, the Genesis story gives voice to a primal human experience of *aloneness* that has existed from the beginning. Reflecting on this passage, we can conclude that as a universal human experience and given its placement and emphasis in the Genesis Creation narrative, the announcement—*it is not good to be alone*—stands out as a statement on the ongoing human experience of aloneness *and* initiates God's salvific response to that human reality.

Here, we move away from the momentum of the biblical text (*one was alone, so God created two*), to focus on the text's salvific question: *How does God accompany humanity in the experience of aloneness?* The point of this question is twofold. First, we cannot arrive at this question until we conclude that the human experience of *aloneness* is part of what it means to be human. It is an ongoing reality embedded in human experience that did not end with creation, hence, it necessitates an ongoing transformational dimension. Second, once we conclude that the creation context of Genesis 2:18 reveals the nature of humanity as both alone and in-relationship, we can recognize God's response as God's active salvific answer to this ongoing human reality.

Accordingly, from the beginning, both alienation and relationality are named as fundamental to being human. Also from the beginning, God is with us in this reality, beckoning us toward one another. Therefore, *how does God accompany humanity in the experience of aloneness? God moves us into deeper relationality with one another.*

Thus, in this scene, a salvific movement surfaces: from the experience of isolation, to giving voice to this suffering, to nurturing this painful narrative toward relational communion, to breaking open the earth creature, to the creation of two, to a jubilant participation in human relationality, and finally, to the realization that "the man and his wife were both naked, and were not ashamed" (Gen 2:25).

The Dance between Aloneness and Relationality

The relationality pronounced in the Genesis story did not end the human experience of *aloneness*. It remains part of who we are, and as part of who we are, it must also possess a transformative dimension and contribute to our salvific potential. In this, we recognize that embedded in the experience of aloneness is the human need to utter, express, and expunge that experience from its internal hiding place. It is this expressive quality in aloneness that often initiates the salvific movement toward each other and God.

Through utterances and expressions, we know that experiences of aloneness, isolation, and alienation are painful. We suffer through these experiences, and the experiences, like in the Genesis story, tell us, "It is not good." Yet here, too, is where we recognize the partnership between aloneness and relationality, for in the act of expressing our pain, we turn toward others, we invite others into our darkness, we fall into the arms of loved ones, we cry out, "Lord, save me!" and we surrender to a cosmological whole—one that is good.

Notably, we must not view this salvific movement as a single conclusive trajectory toward wholeness, but rather as a back-and-forth movement, witnessed as a beautiful dance between Creator and created.[16] By recognizing the back-and-forth dance, we are able to reject the shame and self-hatred that arises when we return to our painful brokenness, and proclaim instead the beauty of our frail humanness and our capacity to stay in the dance.

In a masterful way, the Genesis Creation/fall story captures this dynamic dance. The Genesis story is a beautiful tale of love, intimacy, separation, fear, longing, expulsion, and unending union. In each scene, we see human beings struggling, and we see God's never-ending nearness, demonstrating God's persistence in love and salvation in the human landscape. A brief outline of the plot points illustrates this salvific dance:

1. Humanity is created out of love and for love (Gen 2:7).
2. *Aloneness* is uttered in the context of creation as something "not good" (Gen 2:18).
3. Humanity is complete when two are created, and in their nakedness, they felt no shame before each other and before God (Gen 2:21–23).
4. They eat from the fruit of the tree of knowledge, which is an act of separation from God and contrary to the relational identity of humanity (Gen 3:6).
5. The resulting disconnected self-image is experienced through shame, fear, hiding, and blame (Gen 3:7–13).
6. God searches for humanity in response to their brokenness, calling out, "Where are you?" (Gen 3:8–9).
7. The lack of the permanent state of relationality is evident in God's expulsion of the man and the woman from the garden (Gen 3:23).
8. God's ongoing presence is manifested in the making of clothes for the man and the woman: "God made garments of skins for the man and for his wife, and clothed them" (Gen 3:21).

From this beautiful Hebrew story, the back-and-forth tension between relationality and aloneness is dramatically played out. We continually see God's response to their experiences of shame, fear, blame, and hiding (hiding, as an intended separation from others, is the real sin in the story). In each moment, God affirms

God's nearness to them through the physical salvific acts of walking, searching, calling out, asking questions, remaining present in their experience of exile, and weaving clothes.

Perhaps Julian of Norwich pondered the very sacredness of God weaving clothes when she said, "I saw that he is to us everything which is good and comforting for our help. He is our clothing, who wraps and enfolds us in love, embraces us and shelters us, surrounding us in love."[17]

Ultimately, through the magnificence of this divinely inspired story, we not only see that God's love is unending, but how God acts to make that love known. As *imago Dei*, this, too, is recognizable in our own nature and manifested in our daily lives. Following the Genesis Creation/fall story, this salvific essence is manifested through our innate relationality animated by love; a shared experience of aloneness connected to a shared longing for relationality; our capacity to stay in the dance; our need to be broken open so that transformation can take place; a jubilant participation in each other and God; and our inclination to move toward each other through the physical salvific acts of touching, walking, searching, calling out, and clothing. This is our God with us and for us, and this is the salvific essence that God has made in us.

In contributing to the spirituality embedded in the Genesis stories, *longing* appears as an innate human experience bound to the salvific essence alive in each person. This basic human experience stands out as a primary narrative within each person connecting our innate aloneness and relationality to what spirituality means for each person, especially young people. It is in this connection that spirituality becomes an experience of *longing* within the human context of salvation.

The Holy Longing

In its most basic form, human *longing* represents the inner desire to belong, to be connected, and to find relief. We feel *longing* in our gut, at the core of our being, which often erupts in our deepest sighs, in our nighttime dreams, and in our yearnings for companionship. For this reason, longing can be understood as a central narrative theme, which animates our spirituality.

Longing, as described by Ronald Rolheiser, is a powerful reality that defines our spirituality. Rolheiser writes,

> Whatever the expression, everyone is ultimately talking about the same thing—an unquenchable fire, a restlessness, a longing, a disquiet, a hunger, a loneliness, a gnawing nostalgia, a wildness that cannot be tamed, a congenital all-embracing ache that lies at the center of human experience and is the ultimate force that drives everything else. This dis-ease is universal….Sometimes it hits us as pain—as dissatisfaction, frustration, and aching. At other times, its grip is not felt as pain at all, but as a deep energy, as something beautiful, as an inexorable pull, more important than anything else inside us, toward love, beauty, creativity, and a future beyond our limited present. Desire can show itself as aching pain or delicious hope. Spirituality is, ultimately, about what we do with that desire. What we do with our longings, both in terms of handling the pain and the hope they bring us, that is our spirituality.[18]

These words inspire me to breathe deeply and reflect on the presence of this "aching pain and delicious hope" wrapped in my experiences of *longing*. I'm equally drawn to the notion of the universality of *longing*, as an experience we all share, especially as it relates to our participation in salvation on earth. This is particularly relevant given the *already-but-not-yet* theme in the understanding of salvation.

Scripture scholars have long recognized the tension in the New Testament communities between the kingdom of God now and the kingdom not yet fulfilled in Christ. For example, Jesus preached, "The time is fulfilled, and the kingdom of God has come near" (Mark 1:15), and yet we also hear later in other passages, such as 1 John 3:2, "Beloved, we are God's children now; what we will be has not yet been revealed."

Such passages represent the tension between the divine presence in humanity and the incomplete nature of human existence. It makes sense, then, that since salvation in Christ cannot be fully experienced in human existence, the experience of human *longing* exists as a symbol of this aesthetic reality. While *longing* symbolizes the experience of incompleteness, it also symbolizes the hope in an experience of the beautiful, and a glimpse of the fullness in Christ on earth. As described by Rolheiser, the pain and the hope, the restlessness and the beauty (the *aloneness* and *relationality*) are irreducible partners that make up a reality that pulls us toward love, toward our salvific essence experienced in Christ.

Therefore, *longing* is witnessed as that which moves the person toward expression. It is that inner part of us that can't help but pull us toward human connectivity with others, with God, and with our deepest selves. Like the expressive character in aloneness, longing also embodies an expressive character that draws us toward each other. Consequently, *longing* and the narratives that represent it reveal both the salvific nature we all possess *and* the necessary expressive character that contributes to how we are salvific beings.

Ultimately, based on the reflections and statements proposed in this chapter, we can fundamentally claim that *all narratives are salvific.* Yes, all narratives in the lives of young people are salvific. They are pieces and fragments of their lives that fall within the dance, within the spectrum between the human experience of *aloneness* and *relationality*; they are expressions of the longing, pain, and beauty hidden and manifested in their everyday lives; they exist within the gaze of God's love and mercy; they reveal the connected and disconnected nature of who they are; and they embody their desire to love, to be whole, and to be reconciled to loved ones and to God.

Inspired by this central proclamation, four key narrative themes alive in the lives of Hispanic young people today will be explored in the following part. Each narrative theme reminds us that the urgings by God are still alive today in our young people evident in their painful experiences of alienation, and in the beauty, joy, and kinship alive in their everyday existence.

Part II

❧ ✦ ☙

SALVIFIC NARRATIVES IN THE LIVES OF HISPANIC YOUNG PEOPLE

*T*he previous discussions concerning *narrative* and *salvation* come together here as a backdrop for the real-life stories of today's young Hispanics. Above all, the narrative pieces and fragments that shape and signify who they are and how they are relational are at the heart of a narrative approach.

The following narrative themes represent the dimensions of everyday life that stand out as identity markers and have surfaced as narrative pieces in need of our attention and care. By encountering these narratives, we enact a process in which we enter into the realities that animate their lives, which, in turn, animates the salvific meaning of our lives together.

Likewise, by entering their everyday lives, we come to recognize our role, causing a shift in our perspective that, at times, compels us to respond to the societal realities that—mindful of the pervasive discriminatory environment under which young Hispanics must live out their daily lives—persist in neglecting and demonizing our young people.

In her dissenting opinion opposing the decision to strike down Affirmative Action, Supreme Court Justice Sonia Sotomayor gave voice to this important narrative surrounding the nation. She boldly proclaimed,

> And race matters for reasons that really are only skin deep, that cannot be discussed any other way, and that cannot be wished away. Race matters to a young man's view of society when he spends his teenage years watching others tense up as he passes, no matter the neighborhood where he grew up. Race matters to a young woman's sense of self when she states her hometown, and then is pressed, "No, where are you really from?" regardless of how many generations her family has been in the country. Race matters to a young person addressed by a stranger in a foreign language, which he does not understand because only English was spoken at home. Race matters because of the slights, the snickers, the silent judgments that reinforce that most crippling of thoughts: "I do not belong here."[1]

In her statement, we hear the small stories, the everyday instances that often go unnoticed but are woven into the realities and identities of young Hispanics today. Collectively, these snippets represent the narratives of injustice, humiliation, and marginalization that link the lives of young Hispanics and, therefore, must be named at the onset as an overarching narrative theme: *Race Matters.*

This inescapable narrative hovers over each of the four salvific narrative themes presented in part 2, whether it is made obvious in each or not. Sotomayor's words serve as a reminder to pastoral leaders telling us that today's young Hispanics (along with other young people of color) face systems, institutions, and attitudes that push against the dignity and value they possess, and the health and access that are their right. This is the starting point for them, which differs from others who neither need worry about nor contemplate the color of their skin or the country from which they came. This disparity must continually influence pastoral leaders in our efforts to understand the unique narratives in the lives of young Hispanics, as it is our responsibility to remain aware of and fight against the destructive societal narratives that hinder their chance for a full life. By uncovering these narrative themes, we raise further awareness of the ways in which *we matter*—around what it means for pastoral leaders and the faith community to step into their lives and truly walk with them toward salvific wholeness.

Representing the daily lives of Hispanic young people, part 2 gives voice to several fundamental narrative themes: *The Identity Narratives, The Generational Narratives, The Language Narratives,* and *The Transformation Narratives.* Pastoral leaders are also encouraged to read additional key narrative themes: "The Somatic Narratives," "The Relationality Narratives," and "The Alienation Narratives," available online at https://www.ctr4ce.com/pages/bidss.

As you read through and reflect on these important narratives, imagine the ways in which your own life and the unique lives of the young people whom you serve connect with and/or are distinct from each theme. In this way, the capacity of each narrative to connect to others is enlivened by your stories and expanded into larger narratives that symbolize our communal link.

4

The Identity Narratives

"I Am from Nowhere"

*I*t doesn't take long to be caught by the loving spirit and beautiful people at Dolores Mission. Most people in this community face the daily effects of poverty and violence, especially young people who are affected by at least one of the major local gangs. Yet, while many Boyle Heights's youth are vulnerable to the effects of gangs and gang culture, most are not gang members. Given this dynamic, I learned early on to see all young people as ones living in one communal context best described as *street life*,[1] like what others might call *el barrio* or *the hood*.

Out of this context, I grew to know many young people, some who quickly gave me sage advice: "If you are ever walking down the street and someone stops you or pulls up in a car and asks, 'Where are you from?' you have to say, 'I am from nowhere.'" They explained that what they are really asking is if you live in a rival neighborhood or belong to a gang. Coming from somewhere, from different streets, makes you an enemy and puts your life in danger.

For these youth, this is their daily means of survival—to proclaim that they are from nowhere. They profess this because they don't want to get caught up in gang life; still, they live in the peripheries, on the outskirts of societal care, and it is the question, "Where are you from?" that speaks to these realities.

As is commonly known, you don't just join a gang, you are initiated by some violent means, which may involve getting jumped-in (beaten-up) by gang members. While some youth seek to be initiated, others are targets. From what I understand, as the gang relentlessly beats you, they yell out, "Where are you from?!" "Where are you from?!" to get you to name and claim that you are now from their gang, and they keep beating you until you yell back, "I am from _____ (gang)!"

Growing up in this context, the awareness of knowing *where you are from* takes on new meaning beyond simple city or ethnic identification. It is an identity statement that tells others where you belong, to whom you are bound and to whom you are not. Thus, the proclamation from these youth that "I am from nowhere" is not to say that "I am nothing" or "I don't belong to anyone," but to say that they have come face-to-face with the power of identity, and they know what it means to be bound to others in life-giving and life-threatening ways. From an early age, street life has taught them that identity is everything, and who you identify with often has dangerous implications, blurring the spaces where a young person feels safe, protected, and part of something.

Wrapped in their identity, we can also glimpse the narratives that provide a sense of self-worth, belonging, personal empowerment, and respect, as well as reveal connections to fear, violence, shame, and societal ills. Enacted in a street-life context, these glimpses of identity are especially evident within their symbolic world.

For these inner-city youth, their symbolic world comes alive in relation to their unique bodily identity: in posturing, walking styles, tattoos, hand signs, aggressive interactions such as *cariño*-fighting, expressions of kinship, and intimate greeting rituals. Other symbolic forms related to street life include nicknames, style and color of clothes, hangout locations, street names, numbers, tagging symbols, art work, and codes related to honor, shame, and respect. Of course, symbolic forms and images related to culture (Mexican-Aztecan images), religion (*La Virgen* images, wearing of rosaries), and language (mixture of Spanish, English, and street life terminology) also contribute significantly to the expressed street identity of the youth of Boyle Heights, which will be discussed later.

This brief illustration represents the predominance of symbolic actions and forms related to identity, specifically as they connect to street life. While we can identify similar symbolic elements in other geographic and social contexts, the Boyle Heights's example demonstrates this symbolic world at work given the obvious role that identity plays in the lives of these young people. As such, by recognizing the symbolic elements in their lives, we gain insight into the connections between these symbolic (narrative) pieces and the realities of street life (poverty, fear, violence, discrimination, lack of societal rewards, incarceration, disenfranchisement, injustice, neglect, and so forth), while also recognizing potential connections and disconnections between them and other life-giving sources, such as friendships, family, community, the faith community, and societal care.

In this context, another narrative theme appears that represents the in-between dimension of identity. Note the in-between nature of their existence: living between gang life and everyday street life, living as part of community but left out of the common good, living between migrants' generations and their U.S.-born or raised identity, living between fear and kinship, and between "I am from nowhere" and "I am someone." Above all, this in-between dimension affects identity and reveals the realities at work in their longing and efforts simply to belong.[2]

Belonging is the third major theme and shows up in street life just as in any other context, revealing the hope that these youth are worthy of belonging to something communal that provides care, protection, and love. As a theme, belonging is everywhere we find identity, from inner-city to rural communities, in fact, in each setting where young people are present. To illustrate the importance of belonging, let us consider the identity narratives of young Hispanics living in Central California.

The Belonging Narrative

In the summer of 2015, I gathered a dedicated team of parish music ministers to organize a summer music camp for the youth of the Diocese of Fresno. Serving a predominantly underresourced Hispanic population, the camp attracted over fifty young artists with a diversity of talent, including vocalists, drummers, pianists, guitar and bass guitar players, trumpeters, flautists, and violinists. Ranging from twelve to eighteen years old, the youth attended rehearsals, master classes, and group tutor sessions each day, while also enjoying the swimming pool and hiking trails at STYCC.

Engaging the youth over the four-day camp, they possessed an amazing artistic talent but had not yet had an opportunity to let it shine. Many appeared shy and unsure about their ability, yet they courageously stepped into each rehearsal and performance eager to learn, laugh, and offer their gifts. Over the course of the camp, friendships were built, and they grew to trust each other, which created a brave vulnerability among the youth. This was most evident as they encouraged each other to participate in the talent show, where even the shiest ones stepped alone onto the stage.

I recall a thirteen-year-old girl, Olivia, nervously performing a piano solo and wincing each time she hit the wrong key. Yet, with each wince came voices from the crowd, "Good job, Olivia," "We love you, Olivia." Struggling through it, she stood up as she completed her piece and timidly turned to the crowd. To her surprise, she was immediately greeted with a standing ovation filling the room with clapping and cheers. You could see the disbelief in her face, as she broke down crying, overpowered by the feelings of love, acceptance, and belonging. Several of her newfound friends even rushed onto the stage to embrace her and assure her that she was loved.

This sense of belonging and love was evident throughout the talent show and permeated the entire camp. At the end of the camp, with everyone sitting in a large circle, each youth took the opportunity to share something about their experience at camp, many crying as they did so. One by one, they spoke about not fitting in at school, feeling unworthy and alienated; they spoke about feeling valued, loved, and accepted at this camp; and they spoke about their love for each other, the gratitude for their new friends, and the empowering experience of belonging.

The adults also spoke about the inspiration we gained in experiencing the overwhelming care and love they shared among each other; we spoke about the transformative beauty and sacredness we experienced in hearing their music; and we spoke encouraging words in hope that they trust the beauty of who they are and continue to let it shine.

Much like the story of the youth of Boyle Heights, underneath this story lays the powerful role of identity in the lives of young people living in Central California. In witnessing their struggles to grasp and express who they are, we saw glimpses of their self-image, of their need to belong and feel valued, and of the relational dynamics that can empower and destroy their self-worth.

Again, we are confronted with the significance of belonging and self-worth as major narrative themes of identity. These themes appeared as quiet voices, downward looking eyes, and in the hidden and shy demeanors of many of the youth. Yet they bravely stepped into this setting both nervous and eager to share their gift, which also calls attention to the symbolic world connected to their sense of self.

Music is certainly a symbolic language of the soul, evoking affect, emotion, and communion with something more. Committed to this artistic expression, we could see this soulful language erupt from their instruments, voices, and facial and bodily expressions, as they strained to emote every ounce of feeling. In these moments, they were free from self-judgment, and fully open and vulnerable to their beautiful essence that longed to be expressed.

Then, for some, the glimpses went away and the insecurity reappeared, like an internal judge accusing them of not being good enough. Much like the back-and-forth movement in the Creation/fall story of Genesis, we witnessed a dance from self-doubt to being fully alive, which thankfully found resolution and relief in the experiences of communal belonging.

In the street life of Boyle Heights, this movement was noticeable in the kinship shared between friends, often originating as a counter to the external violent forces in the neighborhood. Here in the music camp, this movement appeared as a counter to the internal voices that told them they are not good, not worthy, and don't belong.

Acting on their true relational identity, the music camp youth responded to each other with compassion, affirmation, and love. In their tender care for one another, they revealed the life-giving essence of a young person's identity—it is not the perfection of giftedness that makes you good, you *are* the gift that is good.

Overall, in both stories we witnessed the power of identity connected to life-giving and harmful narratives, and we witnessed the salvific movement alive in who they are, from "I am from nowhere" to "I am someone," and from unworthiness to communal belonging to stepping onto the stage alone.

Ultimately, these stories tell us that the self-understanding of young Hispanics today influences how they relate to the world and affects their ability to navigate daily life, experience belonging, and engage in relationships. Therefore, by giving voice to how young people understand who they are, we can recognize the narratives at work and the interconnected nature of identity development. As that happens, we can contribute to the resiliency of young people, that is, the life-giving development of who they are and how they perceive themselves. Consequently, we can accompany and assist in empowering and bringing light to their inherent beauty, value, and salvific nature.

Giving voice to these narratives is critical to the function of ministry, since, as revealed in the music camp story, feelings of unworthiness and self-doubt are pervasive sentiments experienced by today's young people. For many, this embedded self-belief inhibits their ability to engage in life-affirming experiences, and, even more so, as evident in the context of street life, reveals the damaging effects of the discriminating and alienating social systems that surround them. In other words, while an internal psychological, cultural, and spiritual dimension exists related to identity, persistent external daily circumstances often promote and sustain the devalued sense of self for young Hispanics today.

The development of a healthy identity is crucial for everyone, especially for young people who are disenfranchised from systems intended to benefit them, such as education, justice, police protection, healthcare, employment, and so forth. Such disenfranchisement contributes to how young Hispanics view themselves, particularly as they affect their experiences of, and hope for, healthy living, safety, perceived value by others, and future possibilities.

Given the persistence of dysfunction and discrimination in these social systems, our attention on giving voice to, and assisting in the formation of, the identity of Hispanic youth is crucial, especially since these debilitating factors shape the development of their identity and serve as markers for us in recognizing the influences in their surroundings that affect their well-being and fullness of life.

Consequently, to embolden our capacity to nurture the identity of our young Hispanics, we must also step into the composite of familial narratives, specifically those related to culture, acculturation, and family dynamics. In understanding these crucial narratives connected to identity, we gain further insight beyond what we observe as we begin to view the larger narratives shaping the core being and self-understanding of the Hispanic young people in our communities. To contribute to the understanding of these narratives, we will highlight the challenges affecting cultural and familial identity related to the process of acculturation.

The Acculturation Narrative

For Hispanic families, confusion and suffering related to identity affects each member of a family differently, evident in the unique experiences of immigrant generations and the first U.S.-born and/or raised generations. Parents and children struggle in their own way to navigate U.S. social systems, while feeling tension between cultures and the desire to belong. Such struggles and desires contribute significantly to a sense of self, especially in relation to the process of acculturation.

Acculturation is the process a person undergoes in integrating another culture with one's own culture of origin.[3] Acculturation is not innately harmful, nor does it suggest assimilation, which infers the loss of the characteristics of one's culture of origin. Still, the process of finding one's self while living between one's Hispanic culture and the dominant United States' culture often generates confusion and stress related to identity and belonging. The *Handbook of U.S. Latino Psychology* defines *acculturative stressors* as "transactions of individuals with both the dominant culture and their culture of origin; these include perceived discrimination and discomfort with adapting to expectations of the dominant culture, as well as feelings of disconnection from the culture of origin."[4] Overall, the potential negative effects of the acculturation process described by the *Handbook* include, "feelings of confusion, anxiety, depression, marginality, alienation, psychosomatic symptoms, and identity confusion associated with attempts to resolve cultural differences."[5]

To distinguish experiences of acculturation within families, it is important to understand that many Hispanic families (grandparents, parents, and children) consist of first-, 1.5-, second-, and third-generation members. The *first generation* refers to the first migrating generation of adults eighteen and older, many enduring arduous journeys to arrive in the United States. Those who migrated under the age of eighteen are considered the *1.5 generation*, since they are foreign born yet mostly raised in the United States.[6] *Second-generation* Hispanics are those who were born in the United States to at least one parent who was born in a foreign country, and *third-generation* Hispanics refers to those who were born in the United States to parents who were the first family members to be born in the United States.

With families consisting of a mixture of generations living part or all their life in the United States, it is understandable that each family member possesses his/her own unique identity, while also sharing similar experiences related to discrimination and the tension between cultures.

First- and 1.5-generation Hispanics are defined by the experience of migration and a strong cultural identification with their home country. According to the Migration Policy Institute (2014 report), of the 42.4 million immigrants living in the United States, 11.7 million are from Mexico, 1.3 million from El Salvador, 1.1 million from

Cuba, 998,000 from the Dominican Republic, and 916,000 from Guatemala.[7] In total, as of 2014, there are 19.3 million foreign-born Hispanics living in the United States.[8]

For first and 1.5 generations, Spanish is their first language (the primary or sole language for many first-generation Hispanics) and many struggle economically and academically, while facing discrimination as they engage the social systems in the United States. A recent Pew Research Center survey reports, "About half of Hispanics in the U.S. (52%) say they have experienced discrimination or have been treated unfairly because of their race or ethnicity."[9] This statistic dramatically increases to 65 percent for Hispanics aged between eighteen and twenty-nine, and decreases to 35 percent for Hispanics fifty and over.[10] Additionally, first- and 1.5-generation Hispanic young people experience tension between cultures as they each struggle to manage daily life successfully, maintain their valued cultural identity, and seek ways to belong in U.S. society.

The 1.5- and second-generation Hispanics are the first generations born and/or raised in a U.S.-mainstream, consumer-driven, social-media–dominant, individualistic culture, while also raised in homes alive with the sounds, smells, images, tastes, and values of a Hispanic culture. They seek belonging, like all youth, yet experience high stress, anxiety, and depression related to negotiating a bicultural/bilingual identity.

For example, since most 1.5- and second-generation Hispanic young people are bilingual (while most parents are primarily Spanish-speaking), they often serve as the "language broker" for their parents, taking on the responsibility of translating, communicating, and representing parents in English-speaking situations.[11] While this fluency in both languages emboldens their identity, it also represents the unique experiences and challenges related to switching from Spanish at home to English at school and other dominant-culture settings. This distinct bilingual/bicultural experience has contributed to the emergence of *Spanglish*, which binds young Hispanics in solidarity.[12]

Additionally, family responsibility (highly valued in Hispanic cultures) sometimes creates added stress and anxiety for older youth who often care for younger family members, especially when both parents are working long hours or work more than one job. Often in these circumstances, older siblings take on ad hoc parental roles, which carry the pressure and responsibility of an adult. The added responsibilities of young Hispanics related to family, including the need to contribute to the economic well-being of the family, often competes with needed time and energy for schoolwork and social engagements with peers, which creates tension and stress within the family.

Such tensions associated with family and the overall acculturation process create stress "on the relationships between adolescents and their parents, which may in turn lead to a breakdown in the familial support systems linked to preventing risk behavior and psychosocial difficulties among Latino youth."[13]

For third-generation Hispanic young people, cultural identity is problematic for those who do not speak Spanish and/or were raised in households where the dominant culture was emphasized. In expressing their Hispanic identity, they often struggle to identify with traditional cultural-religious expressions since these were not central growing up, while also feeling disconnected from mainstream U.S. culture. While each generation feels disconnected in some way, third-generation Hispanics experience a unique sense of rejection or disconnection from their own Hispanic culture. This is especially evident in considering the religious identity of young Hispanics.

Adhering to the religious traditions and sacred meanings of parents and grandparents is a continual source of tension, where expectations often override the need for Hispanic youth to integrate and express their own unique sense of sacred practice and meaning. These familial and cultural challenges between the religiosity of Hispanic parents/grandparents and the religiosity/spirituality of Hispanic young people have been brought to light by recent works.[14]

Hosffman Opsino, theologian and professor of Hispanic ministry and education at Boston College, writes,

> The treasure of Hispanic faith and the people who embody such treasure is not to be taken for granted.

> We must not ignore the fact that nearly 14 million Hispanics, mostly young and U.S.-born, baptized and raised Catholics, have stopped self-identifying as such in recent years. That so many young Hispanic Catholics are choosing not to call the Church their spiritual home matters a lot since approximately 60 percent of the entire Catholic population in the United States 18 and younger is Hispanic. This situation compels us as a Church to turn our attention, with a fierce sense of urgency, toward this important population.[15]

Here, Ospino highlights a narrative disconnection within the cultural-religious identity of young Hispanics, representing both their struggle to uncover and express their unique religiosity *and* their desire to be accepted by and connected to the cultural-religious identity of their parents, grandparents, and the larger Hispanic community.[16]

Ultimately, by exposing the unique experiences of each Hispanic generation, the identities of Hispanic young people emerge. These narrative pieces in their lives symbolize the soil from which their identity emerges and grows. While these narratives, at times, seem disconnected and challenging, the fullness of who they are is equally evident in their beauty, kinship, spirituality, family life, and a life-giving sense of self. Revealed by the youth in Boyle Heights and those at the music camp, the solidarity and care they demonstrated for each other (and continue to demonstrate) proves that *they want to live the fullness of who they are*, as beings created by God to be in-relationship. It is here where pastoral leaders are called to step into who they are by encountering young people where they live and by uncovering how they express their sense of self in hope of belonging to something salvific and communal.

By looking at the expressions, relational interactions, symbolic forms, and generational realities that reveal the identity of young Hispanics, we are given access to their world. We can identify key factors, such as how and where they experience salvific meaning, the ways in which their relationality comes alive, and their experiences of alienation and disconnection. It is from this place that we are not only able to give voice to the salvific narratives alive in who they are but can also consider the ways that we need to accompany and facilitate their movement toward deeper relationality and wholeness, which ultimately involves family, community, faith life, and dialogue between generations.

As this happens, Hispanic young people are better equipped to live the fullness of who they are, knowing that they are held together by ancestors, living family, and community alike, each connecting the experiences of who they are to larger life-giving narratives. This is what is meant by nurturing the identity development of young Hispanics today. Therefore, the following narrative themes are crucial to our understanding of the lives of young Hispanics, as each will continue to uncover the essence, sufferings, and hope of the young people we serve.

5

The Generational Narratives

*A*t its core, ministry with young people is generational—older generations passing on a way of life, a way of being Christian to younger ones. While this transmission of faith is evident in families and cultures (parents, grandparents, and great-grandparents passing on a religious way to younger generations), this process has gained little attention in ministry.

This lack of understanding and investment has contributed to our inability to recognize the narrative break—the disconnection from the generations that have gone before—that has occurred in youth ministry. By failing to consider young Hispanics as part of a lineage connecting them to a way of life, we fail to see the generational composition intrinsic to their personhood. In the absence of this observation, we also fail to see the many ways in which the cultural-religious identity of young people is passed on from generation to generation. Such failings prevent us from stepping into these narratives and contributing to the passing on of faith from within this generational framework.

In recognition of this human lineage, *The Generational Narratives* is presented here to draw attention to the history of a cultural-religious way that has lived on for centuries and now resides often hidden in the fabric of Hispanic young people and expressed differently within each new generational context. Connected to this lineage are two primary interwoven narrative themes fundamental to the generational identity of young Hispanics: The History of

Conquest and Oppression, and the History of Hispanic Catholic Popular Religiosity.

The History of Conquest and Oppression Narrative

The history of conquest and oppression narrative is well established and evident in the centuries of colonization of Latin American and Caribbean countries. It is, for example, in the conquest of Mexico by Spain (1519–21), which has received extensive scrutiny by Hispanic theologians.[1] Such histories are important to recall since they illustrate experiences of violence, annihilation, slavery, separation from families, and the destruction of homes, resources, and sacred symbols.

Describing the conquest of Mexican peoples by Spain, Virgilio Elizondo states, "Masses of persons were slaughtered or condemned to a life of abject slavery and menial labor for the enrichment of others....Violence itself was nothing new to the world, but the extent and depth of the dehumanization stemming from 1492 was, and remains, without parallel."[2]

Roberto Goizueta also recalls a history of violence that cannot be forgotten: "The wounds of Latin American history cannot be erased, for they were inscribed on the faces of its people, in their language, cultures, and religion. U.S. Hispanics cannot escape their dangerous memories, however hard they try; the memories make demands of everyone, including the victims. At some profound level, all Hispanics know that Latin America is the child of violence."[3]

These descriptions serve to remind us of the oppressive history experienced by Latin American peoples and point to the connection of this history to the discriminating and harmful experiences that have persisted for many Hispanic people living in the United States.[4]

Notably, *historical trauma* (HT) theory has emerged in the social and behavioral science fields to help us understand the relationship between such oppressive and alienating experiences and their effects on proceeding generations, especially as it relates to poor physical and mental health. This highlights the scientifically recognized contribution that family history and the history of a people have on the physiological and psychological makeup of today's younger generations. Given its relevance to this discussion on the persistence of oppressive narratives in history and alive today, we will now provide a summary.

Researchers commonly apply HT theory to peoples who have suffered through violent histories (e.g., Native American, African American, and Jewish Holocaust survivors, among others), to comprehend the prevalence among descendants of poor physical health, post-traumatic stress syndrome, depression, psychosocial stressors, and substance abuse.[5]

While it has been difficult to establish with certainty the ways in which trauma and life experiences are passed on to proceeding generations, the field of epigenetics has emerged as a scientific ally for HT theory. Epigenetics refers to changes in the function of genes, which are altered by molecules that attach to genes and affect the production of proteins.[6] The alteration in molecular and gene activity is often the result of significant experiences in the lives of our ancestors, which are passed down to generations of descendants. Ancestral experiences are transmitted through molecular pathways and appear in subsequent generations in psychological and biological forms. The following quote from *Discover* magazine clearly captures the essence of this complex topic:

> Like silt deposited on the cogs of a finely tuned machine after the seawater of a tsunami recedes, our experiences, and those of our forebears, are never gone, even if they have been forgotten. They become a part of us, a molecular residue holding fast to our genetic scaffolding. The DNA remains the same, but psychological and behavior tendencies are inherited. You might have inherited not just your grandmother's knobby knees, but also her predisposition toward depression caused by the neglect she suffered as a newborn.[7]

Proposed by HT theory and epigenetics, we see the bodily realm emerge as the pathway through which ancestral experiences are transmitted intergenerationally, like a memory held in the fiber of who we are, at a molecular level, and passed on to proceeding generations. While this transmission helps us to uncover the negative affects linked to a history of oppression, I highlight this intergenerational connection to spotlight the alternative reality: if harmful effects are passed on to proceeding generations, resiliency and life-giving predispositions must also be transmitted. It makes sense that the data that points to harmful inheritable effects also suggests the possibility that inheritable beneficial effects also exist: "There is no reason to assume that epigenetic mechanisms—which appear to be reversible with appropriate life experiences—would not operate in service to intergenerational resilience as much as to intergenerational trauma."[8] To this point, Professor Karina Walters, director of the Indigenous Wellness Research Institute, calls for further investigation: "Future research should work with tribal communities to identify resiliency responses, resistance strategies, positive coping and other factors that buffered the impact of HT on tribal, communal, familial, and individual wellness."[9]

With these findings comes a new way of understanding the history of generations as we consider resiliency as something passed on intergenerationally. For Hispanic peoples, this has happened through a religiosity that historically was/is experienced and passed on to younger generations, to transform experiences of oppression within communal-ritual experiences of the Divine and each other. Hispanic theologian Jeanette Rodriguez uses the term *cultural memory* to describe this form of salvific communal resiliency. She writes, "Cultural memory fulfills the need to transcend certain events or circumstances (for example, the Holocaust) and/or maintain a corporate identity….This memory passes from generation to generation, from parent to child, from leader to follower, from church to adherent, through oral tradition, written accounts, images, rituals, and dramas."[10] Rodriguez affirms the somatic nature of cultural memory, stating that it is "in our blood," while also declaring that it emerges in affective and intuitive ways: "'Sangre llama a sangre' [blood cries out to blood] is an expression that connotes something in the blood that allows one to access the affective, 'intuitive level.' It surges up without any rational trappings. It has its own truth."[11]

From this framework, persisting over generations, we recognize that historical experiences have shaped the identity of Hispanic peoples, not as defeated ones, but as peoples who have experienced life, God, religion, love, family, and community alongside the experiences of conquest, oppression, humiliation, and discrimination (experiences that persist today for many Hispanics). Linked to *the history of conquest and oppression narrative,* this salvific capacity comes alive in Hispanic peoples experiencing God and defeat simultaneously. By interweaving the narratives of oppression with the narrative of God's accompaniment, Hispanic Catholic popular religiosity emerged as a life-giving source evident throughout the generations, which has served as a primary means of passing on God's accompaniment from generation to generation.

To further explore this fascinating narrative, the following story demonstrates the beauty of Hispanic popular religiosity and its continued influence and practice today. Based on a youth-led *Via Crucis* (the Way of the Cross), the story introduces a deeper reflection to follow regarding this important generational narrative.

The Hispanic Catholic Popular Religiosity Narrative

On Good Friday of 2014, my wife, Patty, and I attended *la Via Crucis* at Immaculate Heart of Mary Catholic parish in Hanford, California. *La Via Crucis* is a Catholic popular religious tradition that derives from early Christian pilgrimages to the Holy Land. Taking hold in the early fourth century, pilgrims traditionally traveled to Jerusalem to walk the passion of Christ, stopping at known sites for reflection and prayer. As Christianity spread and travel to Jerusalem became too dangerous, Stations of the Cross sites emerged in the fifteenth century throughout Europe and Latin America, and *la Via Crucis* soon became a popular tradition for Latin American peoples, still beautifully enacted today, often taking place in the streets in Latin countries and all over the United States in many Hispanic Catholic communities.

Having worked with the Hispanic youth of Immaculate Heart, we were excited to witness their ritual enactment of Christ's passion. The youth in this parish are mostly 1.5- and second-generation Hispanics of Mexican descent and are demonstrably committed to their faith and each other, while also experiencing challenges related to employment, immigration, and cultural identity.

After months of endless rehearsals, the youth began *la Via Crucis* with the intense trial scenes. It was awe-inspiring to see these young people transform into the archetypal characters of Christ's passion. They were each fully committed to their role and truly carried the seriousness and salvific magnitude of the event.

Remaining true to the traditional Stations of the Cross narrative, the trial of Jesus quickly turned to the scourging at the pillar and the carrying of the cross...and so we began to walk.

I can't say enough about that first step—the step that always seems to pull me into this sacred narrative; the step that never fails to unlock waves of emotion and grace. It is here where my narrative becomes one with the passion narrative, where I now take on the role of onlooker, the role of one in kinship with the suffering of Jesus.

Surrounded by soldiers, mourners, and hundreds of community members, we walked with Jesus carrying the cross throughout the large parking lot, which was transformed into sacred space through bodily actions: through the physical act of walking, the wailing of mourners, the yelling by the soldiers, the sight of Jesus struggling to carry the cross, the cracking of whips onto the back of Jesus (not real whips), and the screeches of horror from the crowd.

Stopping to enact each scene—Jesus falling three times, encountering Mary, Simon helping, Veronica wiping Jesus's face, women mourning—I moved to various locations, attempting to get a better view. To my surprise, amid the hundreds walking, I stumbled upon a group of about twenty *abuelas* (grandmothers) singing a song that only they were singing. Afterward, my wife asked the youth leaders if the singing was planned to which they smiled in admiration saying that the *abuelas* organized it on their own.

Walking with the *abuelas*, Patty and I were given a handwritten song sheet, which was copied and placed in a plastic sheet protector. The song, *Perdona a tu pueblo, Señor* ("Forgive your people, Lord"), is a traditional Mexican song sung as the people walk from station to station. This beautiful song symbolizes our plea for forgiveness, "for your deep cruel sores," "for the inhuman whipping," "for the three nails that nailed you, and the thorns that pierced you," "for the three hours of your agony," "for the opening of your side," each with the chorus, "Forgive your people, Lord. Forgive your people, forgive us, Lord."

Walking in their midst, I could see in their faces and hear in their voices the plea for salvation and forgiveness, as this song of the people intermingled with the sounds, shouts, whips, and mourning heard among the larger crowd. I was transformed in hearing this cacophony of sounds, and I found myself singing words that I did not understand but somehow felt at the core of my being.

The air of song and sounds and the shuffle of our feet led us to Calvary as one community, yes, but also as a mingling of generations, traditions, sounds, prayers, and people. Together, we witnessed the crucifixion of our Lord as we prayed and sang, hearing the last words and breath of Jesus—leading us to silence and adoration in hope and preparation for the resurrection to come.

This story illustrates beautifully the grace-filled power contained in creating sacred space built upon an early Church tradition enacted for generations in Hispanic faith communities and now brought to life by the prayers and actions of contemporary Hispanic young people.

This story also draws attention to the continued presence of a Hispanic way of being, brought to life by the *abuelas* through song, highlighting both the matriarchal role *abuelas* embody in Hispanic cultures as the faith-filled wisdom figures who traditionally pass on faith, and the significance of song as the ultimate affective, symbolic expression of the heart. In bringing forth such a traditional song, the *abuelas* gave life to their experience of salvation, which carried a history of meaning for them and for generations of Hispanics. Through their actions, the *abuelas* continued the life of the sung prayer and its ability to transform all of us participating in this unique sacred space.

Noteworthy is that the youth themselves enacted *la Via Crucis* in such a way that they made it their own, which did not necessarily include the song of the *abuelas*. Yet, the integration and harmony generated by both the youth enactment and the *abuelas* song worked beautifully. This was made possible because the communal-ritual life of the community held both together within this fundamental gospel narrative, interweaving the passion and resurrection of Christ with the suffering and salvific life of each member of the community. By stepping into this salvific narrative, the valuing of the uniqueness of each generation occurred as each gave life to their communion with Christ, transforming each into one Body as a result.

While the depth of this discussion surpasses the scope of this book, this simple story from a small Hispanic community in Hanford demonstrates the salvific and transformative quality evident in the history of Hispanic Catholic popular religiosity. Hispanic Catholic popular religious traditions, rituals, and expressions function to create sacred space and evoke the seeing of the relationship between narratives: between the people and God, between my life and your life, between suffering and salvation, and between the narrative of each generation and the larger Christian narrative. It is this relational hinge between narratives that is crucial in understanding the function of Hispanic Catholic popular religiosity. To further explore this relational narrative dynamic, we must go back nearly five hundred years to the quintessential narrative that initiated a host of religious devotions and traditions.

Historically, the archetypal event that illuminates the communion of narratives and its transmission is the appearance of *La Morenita* (Our Lady of Guadalupe) in 1531 at Tepeyac Hill near Mexico City. Out of the depths of the conquest by Spain and the annihilation of indigenous Mexican peoples, Our Lady appeared in sight, sound, and smell, as one who resembled the physical features of a people. Through the senses, the lowly "nothing" Juan

Diego encountered *La Virgen de Guadalupe*, experiencing an affective, sensory, and salvific communion with her.[12]

For Ada María Isasi-Díaz, this embodiment is fundamental in understanding the experience of *La Virgen de Guadalupe*: "Her features are those of the Mexican indigenous population. That divinity resembles them means that the divine is not so far removed from them, yes?"[13] Roberto Goizueta makes this same observation: "The most obvious symbol, of course, is the very color of her skin...her olive skin tells the indigenous people of Mexico that she, *La Morenita*, is one of them. It tells all Mexicans and, indeed, all Latinos that she is one of them."[14] Miguel Díaz contributes to this sentiment, stating, "Guadalupe unveils the face of subjects who comprise the underside of history. Similar to the 'Word made flesh,' who identified with the marginalized, a 'word' of God 'made icon' identifies with a vanquished community by assuming a Náhualt face and communicating through the native culture ethos of 'flower and song.'"[15]

In these descriptions, a picture emerges that signifies *La Virgen de Guadalupe* as one of us, as one who represents, in her being, a communion of narratives, as one who looks like us and enters into our human and symbolic space through the physical characteristics of the people as well as through song, images, flowers, and language.

This sensory and affective archetypal encounter with Our Lady of Guadalupe gave rise to the continued participation in the encounter by bringing it to life for each generation, inspiring a myriad of religious traditions and rituals that have become honored and moving experiences within the overall pantheon of Hispanic popular religious traditions. We see this come alive through home altars, devotions, and street processions celebrating the Feast of Our Lady of Guadalupe on December 12. Contributing to the fullness of Hispanic Catholic popular religiosity, we see similar experiences come alive in the gospel reenactment of Christ's passion (*la Via Crucis*) during Lent and on Good Friday, and we see it in saintly devotions, in our communion with deceased loved ones honored during *el Día de los Muertos*, in the importance of

Ash Wednesday, and in the many traditions surrounding the holy family and the nativity during Christmas time.[16]

Ultimately, through these examples, we see Hispanic Catholic popular religion function as the animator of narratives brought together and experienced at a core level of being, integrating narratives from Sacred Scripture, from history, from the lives of the saints, from Catholic liturgical traditions, and from the life of the people.

From here, we may ask what this means for today's Hispanic young people, especially for the many who do not actively participate in Hispanic popular religious traditions. This disconnection from the life of the faith community and the history of generations is of great concern, especially since it removes young people from a cultural-religious way of being that has historically embodied—and continues to embody—the transformative experience of God's accompaniment.

Of course, the disconnection from religion is, at times, the result of the inability of older generations and faith communities to invest in the realities, contexts, and narratives of today's young Hispanics in such a way that we can integrate their lives into the life of the faith community. While faith communities often do well in articulating the Christian narrative, the relationship between that narrative and the narratives of young people is neglected and often discounted as unimportant.

In response, pastoral leaders are called to enliven not only the narrative themes in Hispanic religiosity, but also what is alive in the fabric of today's young Hispanics; that is, a *longing* alive in their blood, in the core of their being. Here we see the powerful connection between *longing* and the "holy longing," described earlier by Ronald Rolheiser as being fundamental to one's spirituality. We also see something passed on through generations alive in their bones, alive in the *longing* experienced by Hispanic young people today.

By shifting the landscape of ministry to discover the salvific narratives of Hispanic young people, we inevitably discover their *longing* for affective, communal, symbolic, bodily, transformative, and meaningful experiences; ones that bring to life genuine kinship and felt experiences that reflect who they are but that also place their full selves amid love, the Divine, and each other.

Notably, each new generation (consciously and subconsciously) adapts and reshapes the ways in which they encounter these experiences—ways that arise from their unique identities and everyday lives. Consequently, pastoral leaders are called to shift from church space to everyday life, from traditional religious experiences to the new contexts experienced by each new generation, and from known Christian symbols to the symbolic worlds associated with the identity of today's young Hispanics.

By stepping into these frontiers, pastoral leaders are poised to witness the narrative parts, pieces, fragments, and relational spaces that represent the ways that young Hispanics bring to life the salvific essence found across the generations, uniquely involving how they seek to integrate and transform their daily life narratives into larger relational experiences of healing, love, intimacy, kinship, and encounters with the Divine.

Only then can pastoral leaders begin to consider what this means for the role of the faith community, including our response to their *longings* that may appear as fragmented narratives in need of communal wisdom and care.[17]

Overall, the insights raised in *The Generational Narratives* highlight the link between the identity and being of Hispanic young people and a religious-cultural history. Existing in the *zeitgeist* of each generation, stretching back hundreds of years to the present, Hispanic Catholic popular religiosity has animated a salvific communion, uniting and transforming the narratives of alienation and suffering from within the experience of God's love and mercy. As an interwoven whole, these narrative threads have walked alongside each other and have significantly contributed to the cultural and religious identity of Hispanic peoples for generations. Connected to this lineage, Hispanic young people carry this identity with them and seek expression of it, as part of their integration into the salvific communions for which they long.

6

The Language Narratives

"But I don't speak Spanish" is an identity marker signifying that I live in an *in-between space*—I speak English *and* I don't speak Spanish. Only twenty-five years mark the time between my grandmother's migration from Sonora, Mexico, until the time I was born, yet when I speak, my Mexican-ness is unrecognizable to others, especially among first- and 1.5-generation Hispanics. Consequently, I feel compelled to profess my identity in the negative, "But I don't speak Spanish," which is my way of defending *how* I am Mexican. Painfully, I struggle to belong in a world in which the common language is unknown to me, while also feeling different from those who inhabit the Anglophone world in which I am fluent. Hence, while this in-between space marks my identity, it also represents my struggle to live in the *and*—the hyphen—the in-between nature of my existence.

Hispanic theologians have long identified the in-between nature of Hispanic peoples as a source of identity and uniqueness, as well as a source of disconnection. In sharing his story, Roberto Goizueta describes his experience of living between two worlds:

> After years of trying to become "American," and then, trying to become Latin American, I realized that I was not and could never be either: instead, I was *both*, I was *in-between*. Having initially seen my theological vocation as that of building bridges, I now came to realize that, like all Latinos and Latinas, I *am* a bridge. I would now identify with the New York-born Puerto Rican writer who, when asked whether she felt more at home

in New York or in Puerto Rico, responded, "I feel most at home on the airplane."[1]

Virgilio Elizondo also brings life to this in-between reality by foregrounding the historical mixing of peoples and cultures (often resulting from conquest and colonization) as the origin of what it means to be *both/and* peoples. In his work, Elizondo advances the term *mestizaje*, which describes "the process through which two totally different peoples mix biologically and culturally so that a new people begins to emerge."[2] Drawing from his work, Ana María Pineda describes the struggling nature of a *mestizo/a* identity: "The offspring of this union would be forced to live between worlds, on the border of each but never fully in either one. The *mestizo* culture would never be able to realistically claim their root identity on one culture. On either side of the border they would be considered 'different.'"[3]

These experiences of what it means to live in-between cultures, languages, and identity markers, illustrate the realities of many Hispanic young people today. This is most evident in the *bilingual/bicultural* identity possessed by many young Hispanics, indicating they are a unique symbolic mixture (*mestizaje*) comprised of the dominant U.S. culture and their Hispanic culture of origin. As bilingual/bicultural peoples, they possess the capacity to navigate through the language and culture of each, while also struggling to fit in when interacting with first-generation family members, or when visiting their ancestral countries, or with those in the dominant U.S. culture.

It is here that we see the resiliency of Hispanic young people as they seek to enliven their communal nature and shape their identities in such a way that they remain connected to their cultural plurality while also expressing the uniqueness of their in-between existence. Specifically, through language usage, we recognize how they remain connected, experience disconnection, and derive relational meaning from within this in-between space. To explore the substance of these language narratives further, we will consider two narrative themes connected to the bicultural lives of today's young Hispanics: the Spanglish, Code-Switching Narrative and the Monolingual (English) Narrative.

The Spanglish, Code-Switching Narrative

Contributing to their unique identity, Spanglish has emerged as an adapted language form, symbolizing a unique way of communicating for young bilingual Hispanics. Pew Research confirms the prevalence of Spanglish usage among young Hispanics: "As a sign of the times, Spanglish, an informal hybrid of both languages, is widely used among Hispanics ages 16 to 25. Among these young Hispanics, 70% report using Spanglish, according to an analysis we did in 2009."[4]

In studying the mixing of languages by bilingual peoples, sociologists and linguistic scholars often use the term *code switching* to define "the linguistic phenomenon among bilingual people that is marked by the mixing of languages so that a 'word or a phrase in one language substitutes for a word or phrase in a second language'....At times two bilingual people may be speaking for extended periods in one language until one of the dialogue partner's code switches to the alternative language and, without a blink of an eye, continue their conversation in the second language."[5]

In his work related to bilingual liturgy, Jorge Presmanes, OP, advances the understanding of code switching, citing it as an identity marker, a language unto itself. He writes, "Bilingual people might code switch in order to claim a bicultural identity that reflects both the ancestral culture as well as the dominant culture in which they live....In other words, code switching is a language. It is the vernacular of the bilingual and bicultural person. Thus, when celebrated among bilingual and bicultural people, the code-switching liturgy is an inculturated liturgical text in the vernacular of the assembly."[6]

In this context, Spanglish as a form of code switching is recognized as a life-giving identity marker connected to the struggle to belong as in-between people. Here, bilingual and Spanglish usage represents a form of resiliency, especially when placed against the backdrop of historical forces and systems that have sought to discriminate against and, in some cases, abolish Spanish language usage (as illustrated in my dad's story and in the 1968 East Los Angeles walkouts). As "the vernacular of bilingual and bicultural" people, Spanglish embodies what it means to live in this *in-between space*, to belong and to derive meaning with others who share in the experience as *other*. It provides young Hispanics with the means to incarnate, access, and participate in (consciously and unconsciously) their own identity, which is innately joined to a history of generations. With each spoken word and with the ability to switch languages, young bilingual Hispanics can be the *bridge*, as Goizueta says. They *are* the symbol of an in-between culture. They share in the *mestizo* identity of past generations (including the experience of not belonging), while bringing to life their own unique in-between (*mestizo*) identity.

Within this in-between world, we must also recognize the salvific communal life embodied by the Spanish language, which has long been considered a significant symbolic carrier of culture and identity for Latinos and Latinas living in the United States. Ada María Isasi Díaz writes, "The Spanish language functions for Latinas not only as a means of communication but as a means of identification. Spanish has become 'the incarnation and symbol' of our whole culture, making us feel that here in the U.S.A. we are one people, no matter what our country of origin is....The Spanish language for us Latinos here in the U.S.A. has become 'the bearer of identity and values.'"[7] Miguel Diaz affirms this line of thought, saying, "Language is not a tool but rather the closest neighbor that enables human beings to be who they are. Language speaks. It speaks specific human identity into history."[8]

Thus, as a powerful symbol of identity and belonging, the Spanish language represents more than the communication of words; Spanish embodies a way of being that binds people together, revealing a cultural, relational, and affective way in which Hispanics express and receive meaning from one another. It makes sense, then, that among young Hispanics, the Spanish language continues to thrive. This is confirmed by a 2016 Pew analysis that states, "Some 62% of Hispanics ages 5 to 17 and 72% of Hispanic

Millennials speak Spanish at home."[9] Overall, 95 percent of all Hispanics agree that it is "important to them that future generations of U.S. Latinos speak the language."[10]

Still, considering the symbolic value evident in the use of the Spanish language, questions remain related to those young Hispanics who primarily or exclusively speak English. What does it mean to be Hispanic for the growing demographic of English-only Hispanic young people? How does it affect their identity and ability to connect to other Hispanics, especially older generations?

The Monolingual (English) Narrative

English language preference has steadily increased and is sharpest among younger Hispanics, as it is reported that 37.5 percent of Hispanics aged between five and seventeen and 28 percent of those aged between eighteen and thirty-three primarily speak English at home—both age groups increasing 7 to 8 percent in English preference over a fourteen-year period.[11] Substantiating this increase from a generational perspective, a 2013 National Survey on Latinos reports that 5 percent of foreign-born Hispanics primarily speak English, compared to 42 percent for second-generation, and a whopping 76 percent for third-generation and higher.[12] These statistics are especially important given that by 2045, the majority of Hispanics in the United States will be third-generation and higher at 37.4 percent, while 35.7 percent will be second-generation, and 26.9 percent will be first-generation.[13]

Given the rise of English prominence, what can we say about the cultural identity of these young Hispanics? Unable to embody a traditional Hispanic identity through language, are they not considered authentic Hispanics? Have they lost a part of what it means to be Hispanic never to be recovered? While these questions are beyond the scope of this book, we can give voice to the non–Spanish-speaking narrative contributing to the identity of many young Hispanics today.

By no fault of their own, many young Hispanics do not possess the linguistic capacity to express a traditional Hispanic identity and enliven a communion, through language, with other Hispanics young and old. As pastoral leaders, our initial response is to recognize that the loss of Spanish language constitutes a narrative disconnection from a primary means of expressing one's cultural identity, which also constitutes a separation from a history of generations. Aware of this, we must first tend to our young Hispanics who may experience levels of insecurity and shame resulting from this narrative separation. In forming their identity, young Hispanics naturally go through challenges related to identity development, yet the weight of disconnection as monolingual English-speaking Hispanics generates additional cracks not only in the understanding of *who* they are, but also in their search to belong and to discover *how* that identity is expressed and made known.

This disorientation of identity reminds me of Martín, a teenage Hispanic boy who only speaks English and lives in the Central Valley, California. When I met him, he was part of a Catholic youth group comprised mostly of 1.5- and second-generation Hispanics of Mexican descent. He was one of only a few who could not speak Spanish, and I distinctly remember the moment he found out that I, too, don't speak Spanish. His gaze shifted from a shy uncertainty to an upright glimmer. It was as if, in that moment, part of his Hispanic identity was invigorated, and he was empowered to own his monolingual uniqueness, amid others who possess a bilingual identity.

Importantly, my encounter with Martín also revealed an overwhelming sense that he felt that he does not belong. Many young Hispanics today share Martín's story uncovered in that moment, feeling as if they are broken Latinos or Latinas who are different from others and, therefore, viewed as less-than. Unfortunately, many in-between Hispanic young people today overwhelmingly experience this sense of self, including those who are bilingual and Spanish-only speaking. As pastoral leaders, we are called to remain with them in this space, provide a means to give voice to this narrative, and embody a welcoming and affirming atmosphere.

As pastoral leaders, a second response is to recognize the link between language and religion, especially as it relates to those disconnected from the Spanish language. Timothy Matovina, in his comprehensive work *Latino Catholicism*, cites studies concluding that "adoption of English language correlates closely with decreased Catholic affiliation."[14] Drawing from the work of Ken Johnson-Mondragón, Matovina affirms the connection between the loss of the use of the Spanish language and the disassociation with Catholicism, citing "the large gap between the 74% of Spanish-dominant teens who are Catholic and the 57% of English-dominant Hispanic teens who are Catholic."[15] Thus, for many young Hispanics, as cultural engagement declines (evident in the loss of the Spanish language), so, too, does engagement with religion. This reality is substantiated in a 2014 Pew Research Center analysis that reports that while Hispanics constitute the largest demographic of Catholic youth between the ages of eighteen and twenty-nine (recall Ospino's citation: "60 percent of the entire Catholic population in the United States 18 and younger is Hispanic"[16]), 31 percent of Hispanics of the same age (eighteen to twenty-nine) are religiously "unaffiliated,"[17] making Hispanic young people the largest youth ethnic demographic disassociated from Catholicism.

Here, the disconnection with a history of generations discussed in the previous chapter reappears, adding now the absence of Spanish language to the struggle for young Hispanics to connect to the religiosity of their culture. Of course, this narrative theme lives alongside the belief that the cultural-religious identity of their ancestors is alive in who they are, even if dormant, longing to be expressed in other ways. Aware of the effect that language plays in the cultural-religious identity formation of young Hispanics, our third response, as pastoral leaders, is to consider *how* the continuation of language—connected to this identity—might evolve and appear in other ways within the context of their daily lives.

As previously noted, the cultural-religious identity of a people is continuously passed on from generation to generation, while each generation adapts and reshapes cultural elements into unique expressions. Applied to language, this suggests that the cultural life-giving characteristics associated with Spanish language must reappear in other ways for monolingual English Hispanics, most likely in the context of their symbolic-worlds, their bodily identity,[18] and their expressive and affective forms of communicating and receiving meaning from one another.[19] As such, pastoral leaders are compelled to sustain a necessary curiosity around the totality of the lives of young people as the landscape in which their salvific cultural-religious essence is expressed and revealed.

I have earlier attested to this in my life, identifying my symbolic-ritual eruptions as a way of expressing and communicating the spiritual-cultural language in my bones, connecting me to my history of generations. Consequently, I have uncovered a unique in-between narrative alive in my life that has allowed me to link my salvific way-of-being to a cultural way-of-being that is symbolic, relational, affective, and meaningful. Of course, these life-giving expressions do not replace what is lost in my English-only existence, but they do provide a way to incarnate and animate what it means for me to be Hispanic and link me to other Hispanics at a deep level of identity.

My experience points to the possibility that life can find a way to manifest life-giving expressions, which reveal who we are—as unique beings *and* as part of a history of generations. We make this claim knowing that what we find in the lives of young people are often isolated narratives appearing as pieces or fragments, resembling hints of something cultural, relational, and salvific. What we find are narratives that long to be connected to larger narratives designed to animate greater communal engagement and meaning to their lives.

In search of these narratives, the rich associations with language (as an expression of *being, identity,* and *communion* with Hispanic peoples) also function as guides, leading us to find the same elements in other narrative themes, while also reminding us to remain in these narrative spaces alongside our young people—aware that disconnections from traditional salvific expressions such as language and religion indicate the potential appearance of refashioned expressions born out of their in-between lives. Inevitably, the narratives throughout this book represent this possibility.

In conclusion, the language narratives of Hispanic young people compel us to reimagine the scope of Hispanic ministry. To do this, we need to consider that while the Spanish language fundamentally captures the essence of many Hispanics in the United States—and therefore must remain central—we must with urgency and creative energy invest in the diversity of languages and cultures contributing to the identity of the Hispanic young people in our communities. By investing in how young people experience their in-between Hispanic identity, programs and interactions need to expand to include and value each language narrative, as well as the shifts in language usage that occur when praying, and when with the family, with peers, and alone. By investing in these narratives, each young person, from first, 1.5, second, third generation, and beyond, may then feel that they belong and are cared for within the full embrace of the faith community.

Furthermore, Hispanic ministry must draw from all the people of the community to participate as adult leaders accompanying the growth and needs of its youth. This may involve adults who represent a diversity of languages and cultures, including those who do not speak Spanish and who are not Hispanic. From this perspective, Hispanic ministry not only models the full embrace of the community but is also able to serve the entire community as a ministry for all.

7

The Transformative Narratives

*I*magine fifteen Hispanic young people living between cultures, languages, and generations, wanting more from their lives but struggling to find opportunities, support, and resources. They live in one of the most impoverished cities in the country, yet they study hard, work hard, and strive to belong and contribute to family and community. They gather every week to be in solidarity and to live out their faith, seeking to uncover what that means for them and how it shapes who they are. They are a group of young Hispanic leaders that belong to St. Anthony Mary Claret parish in Fresno, California.

As part of the *Identity Project*, I had the privilege of spending time with this group over several months in late 2013 and early 2014. During that time, I got to know them and hear their remarkable stories in response to the identity questions: Who are you? Where do you come from? What are your dreams? Who is your God? In February 2014, during the *Identity Project* retreat weekend, the group created, rehearsed, and performed a short dramatic performance based on the first of these questions. They simply titled it *Who Are You?*

We were amazed by the performance, which wove together their own sense of self with their identity as beloved children of God. The performance utilized contrasts in music, lighting (dark/light), and costume (black/white T-shirts) to symbolize the tension they experience in feeling both unworthy and sinful, and loved and empowered by Christ. The group also masterfully produced a soundtrack including powerful music and voice-overs. Mixed with live voices and lighting features, we were moved and overwhelmed by its message.

While the following description of the action and words does not fully capture the emotion and power of the performance, it does reveal the utterances, voices, pains, and salvific proclamations of these young people.

"Who Are You?"

Young people walk back and forth in a large room, creating an interwoven flow, as they pass by each other in continuous motion. A loud voice-over repeatedly echoes the question *Who are you?* The music evokes the importance of the question, as each youth (wearing a black T-shirt), stops one by one in the middle of the room and responds:

I am a student.
I am an athlete.
I am a musician.
I am a worker.
I am a leader.
I am a dreamer.
I am a fighter.
I am a survivor.
I am a believer.
I am a youth leader.
I am popular.
I am an artist.

As they continue to walk back and forth, Jesus enters the scene trying to get each person to pause and be with him, but Jesus is pushed aside, ignored, and generally goes unnoticed.

After all of the youth voice their response, an ominous voice is heard throughout the room, symbolizing their dark side, like an accuser seeking to destroy their souls.

No, you are a sinner!
You're alone.
You're anxious.

With each utterance, the music intensifies, as does the look on the faces of each young person.

You're regretful.
You're ashamed.
You're lost.
You're broken.

The young people feel each accusation like a stab to their hearts. They stop in their tracks and begin to buckle and cave-in as the accusations continue. This music conveys the doom they feel, as the room grows dark.

You're worn out.
You're bitter.
You're disappointed.
You are unworthy.
You're hurting.
You're invisible.

With great intensity, the voice-over makes the final accusation:

You are all—disgusting!

In complete darkness, the ominous voice stops.

They are no longer walking back and forth but stuck in their pain, unable to move. Strobe lights begin to flicker. They each yell back at the accuser, some internalizing and agreeing with the voice, others yelling at the voice. Their overlapping yelling fills the room with pain and fear.

Jesus is still in the room, trying to encounter each youth. He pleads with each not to hear the dark voice and yells loudly against the accusations. Amid the chaos (all the youth yelling), Jesus proclaims emphatically,

You are not alone.
You are not broken.
You are not worn out.
You are not bitter.
You are not disappointed.
You are not unworthy.
You are not hurting.
You are not invisible.
You are not disgusting!

Silence.

A spotlight appears in the middle of the room, with Jesus and a young person standing side by side. Jesus remains with him, as the youth testifies to his real identity.

You are what? (Ominous voice)
I am a child of the one true King. (Youth)
What does that mean? (Ominous voice)

Each of the other youth step one by one into the light to respond to this question. As they do so, they take off their black T-shirts, revealing a white T-shirt underneath. As each person steps forward, the light grows brighter, as each says, *It means that…*

In Christ, we are all saved.
I have been set free.
I find hope.
In him, I am not afraid anymore.
I am his masterpiece.
I am chosen.
I am transformed.
I have faith.
I am loved unconditionally.
I am deeply known.
I am healed.
I am rescued.

With all the youth now standing together with Jesus, overlapping youth voices are heard in a voice-over echoing for several seconds, saying repeatedly,

Who are you?

The voices stop. All the youth say in unison, while pointing to the audience,

Who are you?

Silence.

As each youth remains steadfast, standing empowered and confident near Jesus, one steps forward, opens a Bible, and reads,

So if anyone is in Christ, there is a new creation: everything old has passed away; see, everything has become new! (2 Cor 5:17).

❦

This transformative narrative reveals the beauty alive in the young people from St. Anthony parish. Through their performance, we become aware of their pain and experiences of despair, isolation, and worthlessness, while also becoming aware of their undying oneness in Christ. In hearing them proclaim who they are, we witness their powerful proclamation of *who they are in communion with Christ*—a Christ who never leaves their side, a Christ who stands with them, warding off the forces and voices that demean and accuse them, a Christ who brings their hidden selves into the light, empowering them to move forward in their daily lives knowing that in Christ they are a new creation.

Through their encounters with Christ, they were inspired to respond to this communion by proclaiming what it means for them: *I find hope; I am not afraid anymore; I am his masterpiece; I am chosen, transformed, deeply known, and rescued.* These truths remain in them and with them, even when they are overwhelmed by despair, and, here, in this performance, we witness these youth stepping into the truth of who they are—ones imbued with God's love and majesty.

Essentially, all they needed from the faith community was a chance to express this reality, a chance to create a prayer, to create an offering of themselves to God. This interweaving of young people, the faith community, and God is at the heart of transformative narratives. In the process of the *Identity Project*, these three aspects combine to give voice to their experiences of Christ.

While not all transformative narratives require deep emotional encounters, *transformative narratives bring together the lives of young people held in support and love by the faith community in the hope of seeing and experiencing new life in a loving God.* While the performance embodies this combination, it also demonstrates the intended effort to join all three, that is, time spent together discussing and interweaving a multitude of salvific narratives. Here we see the faith community and pastoral leaders engaging young people, while also providing the opportunity, the resources, and the inspiration to bring to life a glimpse of what they sense throughout their lives: *that they are more than their individual selves—they are intimately a part of the life of God.*

Recall the examples of other moments highlighted in previous chapters, such as the shared grief during the memorial mass, the creation of the haunted house, the felt kinship born out of *cariño*-fighting, the full embrace of each other at the music camp, the youth enactment of the passion of Christ, the proclamation that "I am from nowhere," in the birth of Andrea,[1] and in the fundraising carwash.[2] Each moment illuminates a deeply felt connection between people that inspired joy, love, tears, kinship, relief, and laughter. Indeed, these moments represent transformative narratives, since they bring to life our relational essence and raise awareness that we are intimately united to one another.

Still, we have also witnessed, in these same moments, narratives that want to be more, that want to be continued into a larger sense of wholeness and purpose, knowing that the life of God always has more to offer and leads us to a greater sense of communion, wholeness, healing, and transformation. Transformative narratives, therefore, are ultimately defined by the experiences that awaken a felt connectedness with life and *inspire more.* They inspire *a response* to the experience and the imagining of, and participation in, new life-giving narratives—ones that necessitate the involvement of the community to be brought to life. This *more* represents the power embodied by transformative narratives, which, in effect, create space for young people to see their lives as part of the sacred world, as part of the life of God. To further illustrate the *more,* as well as the transformative process that reveals it, we recall young Samuel from the scriptures in 1 Samuel 3:1–10.

The Call of Samuel

Now the boy Samuel was ministering to the LORD under Eli. The word of the LORD was rare in those days; visions were not widespread.

At that time Eli, whose eyesight had begun to grow dim so that he could not see, was lying down in his room; the lamp of God had not yet gone out, and Samuel was lying down in the temple of the LORD, where the ark of God was. Then the LORD called, "Samuel! Samuel!" and he said, "Here I am!" and ran to Eli, and said, "Here I am, for you called me." But he said, "I did not call; lie down again." So he went and lay down. The LORD called again, "Samuel!" Samuel got up and went to Eli, and said, "Here I am, for you called me." But he said, "I did not call, my son; lie down again." Now Samuel did not yet know the LORD, and the word of the LORD had not yet been revealed to him. The LORD called Samuel again, a third time. And he got up and went to Eli, and said, "Here I am, for you called me." Then Eli perceived that the LORD was calling the boy. Therefore Eli said to Samuel, "Go, lie down; and if he calls you, you shall say, 'Speak, LORD, for your servant is listening.'" So Samuel went and lay down in his place.

Now the LORD came and stood there, calling as before, "Samuel! Samuel!" And Samuel said, "Speak, for your servant is listening." (1 Sam 3:1–10)

By reflecting on this powerful narrative, we can see more clearly the pieces and processes that contribute to transformative narratives. As in the performance by the youth of St. Anthony parish, it is here that we see the potential fullness of these narratives; the *more* to which the experiences long to be connected.

Specifically, the call of Samuel raises awareness around several key elements consistent with the transformative narratives at work in the lives of young people today. First, like Samuel, the youth in our communities, too, have had, and are having, experiences where they sense God stirring in their lives, inspiring them to respond. In other words, God is already alive in their lives, they are already stirred by God's beauty and love, and they are already experiencing their connectedness to life and are, therefore, inspired to step further into this reality. In fact, ministry is not about inserting God in their lives but about bringing awareness and new life to that reality.

Second, the biblical author sets the scene by letting us know that "Samuel did not yet know the Lord." He did not consciously know God even though Samuel served the high priest Eli and slept near the "ark of God." Consequently, Samuel was not familiar with God's voice, with how God would reveal God's self in the context of Samuel's life. Comparatively, the first man and woman in the Genesis Creation/fall story knew the sound of God's footsteps in the garden. For Samuel, however, while Samuel was able to hear a voice through his senses, he was not able to recognize it as God's.

Like Samuel, many young people today do not recognize God's beckoning within the context of their daily lives. While they are stirred by beautiful encounters, causing them to sense a deep connection with life and others, these experiences often remain isolated, unable to move toward the relational wholeness intended by the experiences.

Third, transformative narratives reveal a connectedness to life, causing young people to see and feel this connectedness deeply. Hearing the voice moved Samuel deeply, causing him to arise in response. His desire to respond, to step further into the experience, led him to Eli. Although Eli did not call for Samuel, Samuel repeatedly brought his experience to Eli's attention.

It is here that Eli enters into Samuel's experience, much like we, too, are called to enter into the experiences of our young people. At first, Eli did not know what was happening. Like many of us, he did not have an answer. Still, Samuel persisted in letting Eli know that he was hearing a voice calling to him and requiring a response. For Eli to recognize what was happening, he had to listen sincerely to Samuel, to hear in his voice and see in his readiness that he was being summoned in a most profound way. Additionally, the narrative does not indicate that Eli heard God's voice—only Samuel heard it. In other words, Eli had to trust that God was calling Samuel *and* that young Samuel was hearing it. Concluding that this was happening, Eli invited Samuel to respond in a most amazing way, knowing that God would never cease calling Samuel.

As pastoral leaders, we must, like Eli, listen, see, and sense the ways in which God is made manifest in the lives of young people, and we must help them to see this reality. We must draw attention to that which we recognize as God's active presence in their lives, beckoning them to step further into life, love, relationships, healing, and wholeness. This is what it means to nurture salvific narratives—to orient young people toward their deepest selves that are connected to God and others.

Fourth, the young people in our communities need wisdom figures and trusted loved ones to orient the salvific experiences in their lives toward a deeper communal participation. Sensing God's intimate call to Samuel, it is significant that Eli did not interpret what God wanted from Eli. Amazingly, Eli simply continued the experience for Samuel by orienting the experience toward something more, by imagining new life-giving experiences that may result from the response, "Speak, for your servant is listening."

Our young people, too, need us to inspire their imagination to consider new life-giving experiences resulting from their relationship with God, with Christ, and with the Holy Spirit. Like Eli, this does not mean that we must immediately apply teachings and moral frameworks to their experiences. Our role is to nurture the experiences by letting them continue to breathe, by trusting the ways in which God appears, and by trusting that our young people are worthy and ready to move forward. Essentially, we must teach them to listen to God's presence in their daily lives and to respond to God's presence in the simple words, "Your servant is listening."

Last, as revealed in the call of Samuel, transformative narratives involve three particular components: (1) a sense by pastoral leaders that God is stirring in their lives even though God is often experienced as a stirring of something not yet known to young people; (2) the recognition that wisdom figures are often needed to raise consciousness of God alive in their intimate experiences with others and with the Divine; and (3) a response inspired by these experiences, which involves stepping further into the communion with God, self, and the life of the community.

The transformative process in Samuel's call inspires us to see ministry from Eli's perspective—one that points to the Divine alive in the lives of young people and steps into these experiences to utter with them the transformative "I am listening." In taking this role seriously, pastoral leaders might organize leadership teams to develop rituals, retreats, and prayer experiences designed to awaken God's presence in their lives and inspire a response through an action, utterance, or naming of their transformative union with God and the community. In small and large ways, we metaphorically set up chairs and created space for the beauty and majesty of young people's lives to be revealed within the context of the sacred, of the life of the faith community. We conclude this chapter with an example of a prayer experience that utilized this interwoven approach designed for the Hispanic youth in Boyle Heights.

A Prayer Experience with Tupac and G

As a Jesuit parish, Ignatian spirituality has long been a staple in the spiritual practice of the Dolores Mission community in Boyle Heights. Enlivened by the poetic meditations written by long-time pastor Mike Kennedy, SJ (pastor 1994–2007), Ignatian meditation is practiced in the base communities, in the leadership gatherings, on retreats, with the eighth-graders at the Dolores Mission School, and is modeled in much of the spiritual activities of the parish. Rooted in the gospel narratives, this form of Ignatian meditation inspires each participant to imagine himself/herself in the narrative, as well as, imagine the Divine reality in the gospel alive in his/her daily life.

With such a proven track record in this community-wide practice, I was eager to witness the lively effect Ignatian meditation would have on the eighth-graders of the school. As the meditation leader of a small group of six to eight eighth-graders, my attention was quickly drawn to the talking-listening dependence of this practice, especially the overreliance on a young person's ability to engage and derive meaning in the narrative solely through hearing the spoken word. On each occasion, most of these young teens appeared distracted, uninterested, and in the follow-up reflections, many were unable to simply repeat what had been spoken. As I observed this spiritual practice with other teenage groups, similar reactions occurred. Of course, some individual youth did experience levels of engagement and meaning. Over time, however, it became clear that something was missing in the mediation experience. Consequently, I paid greater attention to the hidden spirituality of these teens to identify not only how they communicate but also the diverse ways in which they connect to other people.

We set out to create a prayer experience for the teens in the confirmation program, about forty of them, all of whom were about sixteen years old. Based on Ignatian meditation, we designed the experience around the theme *what is my name* since one's name represents a primary theme in Confirmation *and* it has a unique importance for youth living in gang-affected areas.

In 2009, Greg Boyle's book *Tattoos on the Heart*[3] had not yet been published, although he was kind enough to send me a couple of chapters of the manuscript. For the youth in this neighborhood, Fr. Greg (or "G" as he is affectionately called) is revered. As the previous pastor at Dolores Mission and the founder of Homeboy Industries, he is still connected to the community and is known as someone who genuinely loves and walks with them.

After reading Fr. Greg's heartfelt chapters, I was pleased that several of his stories centered on names and on the power involved in hearing one's name. I received permission from Fr. Greg to read excerpts from his chapters to some of the youth.

Standing in a crowded room, with lights dimmed and an empty basket and lit candles placed on a simple altar in the middle, I held up a paper-filled binder and said, "A reading from Fr. Greg."

Silence. Eyes widened. You could hear a pin drop.

As the reading began, you could see the warmth in their faces, as they soaked in the moving stories *from their neighborhood*; stories from their own streets about young people just like them. In hearing his words, they recognized themselves in stories wrapped in hope, compassion, and God's embrace. Here is an excerpt of one of the stories:

Often after mass at the camps, kids will line up to talk one on one. The volunteers sometimes invite the minors to "confession," but usually the kids just want to talk, be heard, get a blessing. At Camp Afflerbaugh, I'm seated on a bench outside in a baseball field and one by one, the homies come over and talk briefly. This day, there's quite a line-up. The next kid approaching, I can tell, is all swagger and pose. His walk is chingon in its highest gear. It's the most exaggerated, cholo stroll. His head bobbing, side-to-side, to make sure all eyes are riveted. He sits down, we shake hands, but he seems unable to shake the scowl etched across his face.

"What's your name?" I ask him.

"SNIPER," he sneers.

"Okay, look (at this point, I had been down this block before) I have a feeling that you didn't pop outta your mom and she took one look at your ass, and said, 'Sniper.' So, come on, dog, what's your name?"

"Gonzalez," he relents a little.

"Ok, now, son, I know the staff here will call you by your last name. I'm not down with that. Tell me, mijo, what's your Mom call you?"

"Cabron."

There is ever the slightest flicker of innocence in his answer.

"Oye, no cabe duda. But, son, I'm looking for birth certificate here."

The kid softens. I can tell it's happening. But there is embarrassment and a newfound vulnerability.

"Napoleon," he manages to squeak out, pronouncing it in Spanish.

"Wow," I say, "That's a fine, noble, historic name. But I'm almost positive that when your Jefita calls you, she doesn't use the whole nine yardas. Come on, mijito, do you have an apodo? What's your Mom call you?"

Then I watch him go to some far, distant place—a location he has not visited in some time. His voice, his body language and whole being are taking on a new shape—right before my eyes.

"Sometimes,"—his voice so quiet, I lean in—"sometimes—when my Mom's not mad at me...she calls me...'Napito.'"

I watched this kid move, transformed, from Sniper to Gonzalez to Cabron to Napoleon to Napito. We all just want to be called by the name our mom uses when she's not pissed off at us.[4]

I closed the binder. There was silence.

The youth were drawn into the story, hearing it as if it was their story, their hard life, and their mom lovingly calling out to them.

We then began to move back and forth between scripture stories and Fr. Greg's stories, pausing between to reflect with sacred music and contemporary music playing in the background. We chose several scriptural vignettes that involved intimacy and the calling of names, drawing from the second Creation story, the calling of Jeremiah, and Jesus's calling the first disciples. As we shifted from Fr. Greg's stories to the biblical stories, we sensed connections were being made, as they recognized their lives in the hearing of the biblical stories. Interwoven this way, they began to see themselves as part of God's story, as they reflected on both their street names and on the name that moves their hearts through the tenderness of their mother's voice.

At the beginning, we asked them to write down their nickname or street name on a piece of paper. Now, we asked them to reflect again on hearing their mom tenderly call out to them and to write this name on the other side of the paper. By this time, we had sensed that everyone was listening, engaged, and captured by the theme and the weaving of stories. We felt the genuine connectivity.

As they reflected and wrote, we played Tupac Shakur's song *Dear Mama*. Surprisingly, some started singing along. Then overwhelmingly almost everyone joined in, filling the room with their beautiful voices. Although the room was dimly lit (for affect), we could see the intimate child-mother communion in their faces and hear the prayer in their voices—a prayer in the form of a song performed by a hip-hop artist, a *thug* from the streets,[5] a prayer in the form of a song they knew as theirs, representing their lives, born out of the same hardships they have endured. It was in this expressive response of singing that we knew that they were receiving, connecting, and experiencing a communion between their lives and something more—something and someone that loves them.

We then invited them to stand and present themselves to God. One by one, without hesitation, each stood up and gave voice to the name their mom utters, saying, "Hello God, this is _____." They shared this name with God and with their peers, as each placed the piece of paper in the basket on the altar. Extending our hands, we prayed over the basket, which was then presented as an offering in the following youth liturgy.

Afterward, we talked about the prayer experience, and many spoke of seeing the connection between Fr. Greg's stories, the biblical stories, *Dear Mama*, and their own lives. They also spoke of the prayer in terms of a felt experience. On a gut level, they experienced something that moved them deeply but that also moved them to respond by presenting themselves to God. I have never witnessed a more genuine prayer by youth in all my years in youth ministry.

In comparison to the eighth-grade example, this prayer experience represented a shift in how we functioned and structured our ministry. While we continued to struggle as most ministry leaders do, the shift represented an effort to maintain the beauty of the community spirituality, while also making it accessible and connected to the lives of the youth in the community. In creating this prayer experience, we consciously sought to link the prayer to their lives, to make it about them, and to shift it to their world.

To do so, we made sure the prayer experience represented them, drawing from the power of their names and their experiences of hearing their name called by a loving parent. We also extended the sense of the sacred by including Fr. Greg's stories and Tupac's *Dear Mama* alongside Sacred Scripture, sacred music, candles, and an altar. Especially in connection to the Tupac song, we widened the sacred to include their symbols, their passions, and their music, which, in effect, created space for them to see their lives as part of the sacred world.

Finally, they made the power of the prayer real as they sung and stood up to say their most intimate name to God and to the community. While we were able to bring their lives into the prayer experience, *they enacted* the transformative essence by responding to the experience, by singing what they were sensing and feeling, and by literally saying to God, "It's me, _____. I'm listening."

Part III

❦✷❦

PRACTICAL STRATEGIES FOR A NARRATIVE APPROACH TO MINISTRY

The primary function of ministry is to uncover and nurture the salvific narratives in the lives of the people of our communities.

*I*often use this opening statement to launch the central premise of the function of ministry. Created in the image of God, all humanity possesses a salvific essence, an innate movement toward relationality, which is manifested in the connected and disconnected narratives that make up who and how we are.

Ministry is best understood from within this salvific movement, deriving meaning and functioning in strategic ways from within this reality.

Of course, in many ways that is already happening, as pastoral leaders bring lives together to accompany young people and enliven their faith in Christ through the life of the faith community. Yet, what is often lacking is an overarching understanding of ministry connected to what it means to be a human being created by God. Without a framework that raises consciousness around the salvific essence alive in every dimension of life, the collective intention to step into the totality of the lives of young people will never take hold, and the perspective that they are already imbued with the divine and occupy sacred space will never be considered in our ministerial praxes.

Considering this, models and approaches built upon what God has created within us are urgently needed. The narrative approach is but one example of such a model.

To advance this model, part 3 centers on twelve strategies that can be integrated into the ministerial life of the community. These strategies illustrate a practical method for a narrative approach, to be adapted and applied, in parts or as a whole, to fit the needs of our communities.

Fundamentally, these strategies involve ways of thinking, acting, and developing relational engagements connected to the salvific essence alive in young people. The real life of these strategies, therefore, is in the salvific nature that each represents. Ultimately, the aim is to draw attention to the innate salvific life of young people in the hope that pastoral leaders utilize strategies and praxes connected to this life.

8

Strategies to See and Give Voice in a Narrative Approach

*A*t twenty-three years old, I received the best advice that has stayed with me over the past three decades. At the time, I had very little experience leading presentations and was asked to give a lengthy talk on a topic that I no longer recall. I was exceptionally nervous and John, a fellow team member, noticed my anxiety. Putting his hand on my shoulder, John said, "Vince, you've done your job; now let God do God's job." Immediately, I fell into a calm state knowing that God was actively present. It felt like a weight was lifted, enabling me to be myself and thoroughly enjoy the experience. Since then, I have passed on John's advice to others and often use his words as a mantra, especially at the onset of big events.

This story captures two basic components that set up our exploration of ministerial strategies. While these strategies fully expand on "the job *we* do," we must profess from the onset that the work we do is built upon God's ongoing active presence and our commitment to "let God do God's job." This adage serves as a challenge to be faithful to God's work with us, in us, and through us. To remain faithful, in this regard, means that we must believe in the salvific work God has done and is continually doing in the lives of the young people in our communities, even if, or especially when, we are unable to recognize it as such. That narrative, above all, sets into motion our efforts to establish strategies for ministry, the first of which announces our trust and gratitude in God's continued presence in our lives.

Strategy #1: Trust the Salvific Essence Alive in Young People

Our ministerial efforts are grounded in the reality that a deep structure exists where the totality of life created by God moves us toward a deeper participation in the relationships that life offers. As pastoral leaders, our first strategy is to trust that this salvific reality is alive and happening in the lives of the young people we serve.

In recognizing this reality, we also recognize an intended salvific process or *movement* (from aloneness to relationality) that can be viewed in its parts as well as a salvific whole. This, of course, does not flow step-by-step, but involves a myriad of ways for young people to integrate their human experiences of alienation into a healing communion with the wholeness of life.

A simple reflection on our own journeys toward wholeness and salvific communion can attest to the clumsiness and to the village of relationships it took (and takes) to bring about our salvific experiences of healing and communion with God and each other. Having traveled these journeys, knowing we are still on a path toward deeper communion, we are able to recognize the salvific essence as a reality alive in our young people as well.

In recognizing this, we enter into their salvific narratives knowing that the salvific process God has created in them involves particular life-giving dimensions that we can identify and trust as part of a salvific whole. These dimensions include seeing, giving voice, naming, foregrounding, raising awareness, integrating lives with the life of the faith community, proclaiming God's kinship, inviting a response, and the imagination of new transformative narratives. Each of these represents a salvific expression that carries the life-giving movement toward true experiences of our connectedness to God and each other. It follows, then, that each dimension also reveals a strategic way for ministry to function and accompany the young people in our communities.

Thankfully, trusting the salvific process relieves us from the overwhelming burden of feeling as if we must figure it all out, and that everything we attempt must have a clearly defined order or outcome. Given the nature of this narrative approach as an investment into the fullness of young people's lives, the salvific process upon which it is built has no clear beginning or end, overlaps in its strategies, and is often messy, unclear, and unmeasurable. This means that we must trust God's salvific essence alive in their lives, while also trusting the creative intuition God has bestowed on us as part of that salvific process; we must trust that God will inspire us with what to do next, with what to do with what we *see*. I say this with confidence, having experienced, time and time again, God's intervention and inspiration for what comes next. From the creation of a haunted house in a violent neighborhood, to the need for a memorial Mass, to the development of a music camp (none of which were preordained outcomes), in prayer and trust God inspires us in the ways in which we walk with young people as they journey along unexpected paths in search of the salvific communions they long to experience.

To that end, these strategies are both a means to bring life to the salvific process imbued in young people's lives and a means to name our participation in this reality as the primary function of ministry.

Strategy #2: *See* How Young People Are Connected and Disconnected

The longstanding strength of Hispanic ministry is that it starts with the everyday lives of the people of the community, a starting point echoed by Pope Francis: "We must always consider the person. Here we enter into the mystery of the human being. In life, God accompanies persons, and we must accompany them, starting from their situation."[1]

This starting point, from *la base*, is the life-blood of effective ministry and is the defining difference between Hispanic ministry and traditional mainstream approaches. Regarding method, the well-known *see-judge-act* process has historically represented this starting point.[2] In particular, the first element—*to see*—requires pastoral leaders to participate deeply in people's lives on the level of kinship, theological curiosity, and *cariño*. In fact, by doing the work of *seeing*, the relational-salvific quality of our ministerial efforts is magnified tenfold.

Yet there is a great need to reinvest in what it means to ground ministry in the everyday life of the people and to renew our understanding of why we *see*, how to *see*, and what to do with what we *see*. This narrative approach represents my contribution toward this endeavor, while also remaining true to the relational dynamic that defines the entire salvific process.

As a strategy for ministry, *to see* means to start with the life of the people: to go into the neighborhoods and homes, to invest time in relationships, to listen, to ask questions, to create space for engagement and dialogue, to go to the peripheries, to be curious, to investigate, to seek understanding, to value everyone, and to learn about the social, economic, and political realities affecting the people we serve.

As pastoral leaders, we are always in the process of *seeing*, since it is not akin to a one-time needs assessment but an ongoing ministerial way of being. However, from that perspective, it may seem that *to see* requires never ending analysis and constant engagement with everyone in the local community. While ideally beneficial, it is not practical to consider *seeing* as an exhaustive investment in everything related to the people of the community.

Consequently, in the effort *to see* our young people, we must first ask this question: What are we looking for? Above all, we are looking for the ways in which our young people are connected and disconnected to the relationships in their lives—to their inner selves, to each other, to the life of God, to their family, to their neighborhood, to the faith community, to their culture, to the fullness of life, and to any other prevalent relational form. This relational foundation is perfectly echoed by Hispanic theologian Roberto Goizueta, quoted earlier and repeated here: "The ultimate goal of all human action is nothing other than the active participation in relationships and the enjoyment of those relationships, wherein the particularity of each person can be affirmed and allowed to flower."[3]

In executing this strategy, several practical approaches may serve as starting points in our efforts to see these relational narratives at work: "*See* Who They Are, Where They Are, and How They Are"; "Location, Location, Location"; "Start with One Thing: Questions"; "*See* What Catches Our Attention"; and "*See* a Particular Theme."

SEE WHO THEY ARE, WHERE THEY ARE, AND HOW THEY ARE

In our efforts *to see* connections and disconnections in the lives of young people, what we inevitably encounter and uncover is *who they are*, which necessarily includes *where they are* and *how they are*. By considering these three areas of concentration, we ensure that the personal, societal, and expressive dimensions of their lives are heard, understood, and nurtured.

Specifically, in looking for *who they are*, we seek to uncover the narratives connected to their identity, narratives including where they come from, their self-perception, their experiences of God, their cultural and religious identity, their family life, peer life, community life, and their passions, shortcomings, dreams, and fears.

In looking for *where they are*, we seek to uncover their geographic location, the social, economic, and political influences related to their neighborhood, the locations where they interact with others (including cyberspace), and the influences of street life and other realities specific to inner-cities, rural areas, coastal communities, and so on.

In looking for *how they are*, we seek to uncover how they express, communicate, and/or hide their relationality, their longings, their identity, their brokenness and sins, their values, and their needs. In looking for these expressive forms, we inevitably encounter their bodily expressions, their symbolic world, their personalities, and their artistic giftedness.

103

As entry points into their lives, these three areas enable us to grasp the dimensions representing the fullness of their lives, while also considering the relational connections and disconnections evident in each specific dimension.

LOCATION, LOCATION, LOCATION

To engage young people within their relational landscape, a shift in where ministry happens must occur—a shift that reflects our belief in God's salvific presence in *la vida cotidiano* (the everyday life), and reflects the awareness that, without this shift, we limit our ability to see and nurture the salvific narratives alive in the totality of their lives.

As a ministerial strategy, location focuses on *where they are* as a strategy to engage young people in their everyday lives, wherever this occurs: in the homes, parks, schools, workplace, alleys, jails, street corners, digital world, sports field, hospitals, coffee shops, and so on. Notably, our interactions in these spaces often challenge us to engage the social, economic, and political realities that influence the lives of our local youth, affecting their access to and support in living a healthy communal-centered life.

Overall, the shift toward daily life and the expansion of ministerial locations within that life must be a priority when considering the salvific purpose and function of ministry. This mandate is strongly promoted in the *Conclusiones* document based on *El Primer Encuentro Nacional de Pastoral Juvenil Hispana* (2005):

> Take the personal, sociocultural, and religious reality of the jóvenes as the starting point for ministry....Bringing the Good News to Hispanic jóvenes implies action outside of the church buildings, the parish facilities, and the weekly meetings. It moves us from the pews to the shoes...seeking out the jóvenes in their homes, their schools, their workplaces, their neighborhoods, as well as the movie theaters, dances, labor camps, and wherever else they live and gather.[4]

START WITH ONE THING: QUESTIONS

While effective ministry begins with the life of the people, our effect increases as we ask questions related to their lives. Questions are powerful, and the use of questions in all facets of ministry and in all interactions with young people is to be encouraged. For example, the *Identity Project* centers on four basic questions: Who are you? Where do you come from? Who is your God? What are your dreams?

Other basic questions might include those directed at pastoral leaders: Who are we? Who is our God? Who are the young people of our community? Who is not here or left out, and why? How can we expand our locations of engagement with young people? Of course, there is a multitude of fruitful questions, but it is beneficial to generate those that lead us to focus on one narrative theme or one location at a time, such as visiting young people in their homes, or focusing on a specific age or gender, or seeking out those disconnected from the Church, or creating dialogue sessions with parents, or talking to school and local counselors and therapists about mental health needs.

By focusing on specific questions centered on one aspect at a time, we move further into one narrative theme. As a result, we engage young people at a meaningful level and create space for further narratives to be uncovered, which of course inspires more questions.

SEE WHAT CATCHES OUR ATTENTION

Seeing often entails a deeper look at something that catches our attention, which may involve youth movements and social activism, new forms and usage of social media, a new fashion or music trend, fear and grief related to local and national catastrophes or events, excitement over a movie, TV show, or book, enthusiasm for a specific religion or spirituality, or uncommon noticeable bodily expressions like *cariño*-fighting.

In each instance, we are caught by something revealed in their expressions and energy, and, in our efforts to see what it means for them, we must look carefully at the manifested relational connections and disconnections by asking questions, seeking understanding, and stepping further into these narratives.

See a Particular Theme

Seeing may include a closer look at particular themes alive in the daily life of young people. Themes such as forgiveness, friendship, prayer, birth, death, food, faith, social media, hospitality, community, justice, and family are but a few of the many themes that reveal the salvific depth that is alive in the everyday existence of young Hispanics.

It is no accident that such themes are also alive in the life of the faith community, since at their core they are relational-salvific themes. Consequently, the rich use of this strategy benefits ministerial programs, since by uncovering salvific themes in the life of young people we enable our ability to nurture each salvific aspect by connecting young people to similar themes examined in religious education, sacramental preparation, faith formation programs, and the liturgical life of the faith community.

Overall, these basic starting points represent the many interactions and approaches that reveal the relational connections and disconnections central to our efforts *to see*. They also initiate the ongoing life of the strategy *to see*, since the work of *seeing* contributes to and influences the life of each strategy. How we *see*, and what to do with what we *see*, will continue as this strategy *to see* develops within the details of all the other strategies.

Strategy #3: Can We Just Stop Talking?

Building a ministerial framework by uncovering and nurturing salvific narratives in the context of the relational essence of young people is a major undertaking. Not only does it require us to slow down and enter into the unmeasurable and unpredictable world of relationships, it also conflicts with the common setting and way in which ministry with youth traditionally happens. Of concern is the talking-listening model of ministry that currently dominates the youth ministry landscape.

Across the United States, Catholic leaders regularly gather with young people in a variety of ministry contexts. It is common practice for these gatherings to take place in classroom-type settings using a classroom-style model, conjuring the image of a teacher talking and students listening. In this setting, led by adults and sometimes youth-aged peer leaders, the primary dynamic is one person talking in front of a group of young people listening.

Given this historic use of the classroom-style model—both as a setting and a didactic method—for catechetical instruction across the United States, it is no accident that this paradigm has a stronghold on the way we currently conduct our youth ministry gatherings. While a study of the history of this paradigm is beyond our scope, there are several issues we can assess regarding this classroom-style model, which can be referred to as the *Adults Talk—Youth Listen* model.

ASSESSING THE DOMINANT ADULTS TALK—YOUTH LISTEN MODEL

The first concern with the *Adults Talk—Youth Listen* model is that it moves only in one direction from adults talking to youth listening. This model of ministry assumes that faith is passed on via a relay of information; information that adults possess and youth lack, so that the role of the adult is to say the right thing, say it in an inspiring way, and say all that our youth need to know to be good Catholics. This role does have a level of effectiveness. However, if we as adults believe that unless the adult says it, they (the youth) won't know it and, therefore, can't live it, then what's missing from that equation is that God is already alive in the lives of our youth in a multitude of relational dynamics; what is forgotten is that life, family, cultures, community, and a history of generations are already prompting growth and experiences in faith.

Here, the relational network involved in how we become who we are as a person of faith and as a community of believers needs highlighting. Given this multidimensional relational network that binds us together and brings faith alive, we cannot simply rely on the *Adults Talk—Youth Listen* model to carry the entirety of something that requires an entire network to be experienced.

By widening our understanding of the peoples, realities, and locations that bring faith alive, it becomes clear that the monodirectional trajectory from adult to youth prevents us from investing in ways for youth to give voice to these salvific realities.

They Talk—We Listen

If the role of the pastoral leader is to talk, then when will the adult ever stop to listen; and if the role of our youth is to listen, when will they ever get a chance to talk? Growth in faith is a relational endeavor, requiring an equal value of one another and the sincere awareness that God is alive in all of us. Our young people have rich lives filled with experiences of God, love, relationships, brokenness, and healing. From this stuff of daily life, the faith of our youth grows, and it is our role as pastoral leaders to walk with them, create space for them to express their lives, and *listen*. Consequently, we discover that the faith of our youth is passed on to us and we, too, grow. I've learned immensely about faith and community from "un-churched" *barrio* kids.

Consider How Youth Communicate and Receive Input

By relying heavily on the spoken word to carry the meanings of faith, the *Adults Talk—Youth Listen* model assumes that the only way in which youth receive messages, information, and meaning is by listening to the spoken word. It assumes that in hearing someone talk, sometimes for long stretches at a time, young people should be able to receive fully the faith-life essence of what is being said. This misperception opens the door for youth to be accused of having limited attention spans or of not caring about their faith, especially if it is perceived that the message did not take hold. It also assumes that the passing on of faith and receiving meaning on a deep level happens in passive, hearing only, no-response-required ways.

This concern is magnified when we realize that, for today's youth, the practice of listening to words has given way to multi-sensory forms and a global digital connectivity. For them, communication is typically image-based, short, instant, narrative, visual, symbolic, and touch-driven. Consequently, we lose context and effectiveness when we assume that listening to the spoken word carries the same investment as it did for past generations. This generation gap is especially evident when we consider the value and effectiveness of oral tradition and the spoken word for older generations, specifically within Hispanic cultures.[5]

Ultimately, the strategy simply to stop talking challenges pastoral leaders to consider the ways in which longstanding models hinder our ability to function effectively as life-affirming faith communities invested in the salvific lives of young people today. In turn, by removing or limiting the *Adults Talk—Youth Listen* model, our dependence on words shifts to a dependence on what God has made and enlivened in the lives of young people, requiring us to *see* the expressive, nonverbal, symbolic, artistic, and bodily narratives that make faith real for them. Consequently, this strategy invites us to activate our primary role to accompany young people in a spiritual awakening that emerges from *their* totality of life.

Strategy #4: Give Voice Always and Everywhere

At its core, to give voice is a salvific act. By giving voice to their lives and by having their voices and expressions seen and heard, young people move from private space to relational space—from inward to outward—and, in the process, gain greater awareness of their value and relational fullness.

Concretely, this reality inspires ways to create space for the narratives of young people to breathe out loud in all manners, forms, and expressions, allowing pastoral leaders not only to *see* the parts of their lives that the young people reveal but also see the depth of narratives linked to them.

Our goal, then, is to give voice always and everywhere in all facets of ministry. To invest fully in this strategy, pastoral leaders are prompted to (metaphorically and literally) stop talking and place the voices and expressions of young people at the center of our engagements with them. Here are four practical approaches to assist with this endeavor. They are "See *How* They Are Already Expressing Who They Are," "Create Space to Give Voice," "See It Elsewhere," and "Naming."

See *How* They Are Already Expressing Who They Are

Before we create space for youth to give voice to who they are, we must first see how this is already happening and identify the expressive and communicative forms they are using. Here, we emphasize forms of communication and expression because (a) they are tangible and recognizable, (b) they lead to the discovery of narrative connections and disconnections related to the form, and (c) when creating space for young people to give voice, our effectiveness in ministry increases when we draw from the forms of communication and expression they value.

In the second part of the book, we highlighted many forms of expression that consciously and unconsciously voiced who they are. Some of these included *the act of walking* connected to la *Via Crucis* in Hanford, California, as well as the street life and religious identity of youth living in Boyle Heights;[6] *cariño-fighting* as a bodily expression of their longing to experience a felt-kinship, while remaining disconnected from the transformation narratives alive in the faith community; *Spanglish* as a linguistic form representing the cultural in-between nature of their lives and the connections and disconnections between the culture (and country of origin) of their parents and U.S. mainstream culture; and *music* as a symbolic expression of their daily life that carries the potential to connect them to larger communal narrative themes, as we noted in the "Tupac and G" prayer experience.

Of course, many other forms of expression exist that serve to give voice, including social media, fashion, graffiti, dance, poetry, art, tattoos, bodily mannerisms, and gathering places like parties, protest rallies, support groups, faith-based gatherings, and twelve-step programs. Each represents their way of saying, *This is who I am*, *This is what I value*, *This is how I suffer*, and *This is what I need*.

Nevertheless, the youth themselves are not always fully aware of the depth of meaning and connectivity that their expressions contain. Consequently, seeing how they are already voicing/expressing only begins the strategy to *give voice always and everywhere*, since our role as pastoral leaders is to nurture these expressions toward consciousness and deeper communion.

CREATE SPACE TO GIVE VOICE

The strategy to give voice involves creating opportunities for young people to express themselves in every way possible. This emphasis highlights the need to create safe and sacred spaces for the narrative pieces of young people to be expressed within a consciously constructed larger context. Therefore, creating space inevitably invites young people to breathe out loud in spaces that involve familiar and trusted adults and pastoral leaders.

Such spaces can be as basic as a park bench, chairs in a room, religious education settings, weekly youth gatherings, liturgical events, or they can be created through the collaboration on major projects, such as an artistic project (like a mural, film, or the Identity Project), a constructed ritual (like *The Boat*), or a retreat activity (like a reconciliation service or obstacle course). In creating such spaces, we empower the ability of young people to give voice, especially when we utilize the communication and artistic forms they value. Thus, we bring a piece of their lives into a larger salvific space and promote their ability to see themselves connected to it.

Here, pastoral leaders are given the opportunity to design spaces that invite young people to express themselves (verbally, artistically, and physically) within a salvific context. The beauty of these spaces is that as young people bravely express pieces of their lives, we are present to see it, hear it, and receive it. While this on its own is salvific, we have the added opportunity to place these encounters within the embrace of powerful Christian narratives and the life of the faith community. Young people are held together by larger salvific narratives every time we take powerful scripture narratives and Christian themes (e.g., forgiveness, initiation, grief, family, prayer, and social justice), and create opportunities for their unique lives to be expressed within that context.

Finally, dialogue circles are effective in allowing young people to articulate, reflect, share, scream, cry, laugh, and ask questions. As noted earlier, here is where I have found my most meaningful purpose: to set up chairs, buy pizza, and listen. Whether based on a specific theme, a tragedy that needs to be processed, a mixing of generations, or just a chance to engage, each dialogue circle is an intermingling between youth and adults that often exposes deep-seated emotions and experiences, requiring further attention and inspiring further opportunities. In the following chapter, foregrounding (as a strategy to bring what is hidden into relational space) is used to continue the narratives fragments that are exposed in the process of giving voice.

In creating space for youth to express their lives, we help raise their awareness of the unique beauty and inherent value they possess. We also raise our own awareness of the depth and totality of their lives, thus inspiring us to step further into their salvific narratives to which they give voice in the spaces we create.

SEE IT ELSEWHERE

In facilitating young people to give voice to who they are, it often helps to center on certain narrative themes as points of reflection. This is typically the case in religious education, faith formation, sacramental preparation, and retreat settings. To assist them in seeing and giving voice to these themes in their own lives, the *see it elsewhere* approach can be useful.

This approach challenges pastoral leaders to find examples of salvific themes in movie clips, artwork, YouTube videos, scripture stories, our personal lives, the lives of the saints, modern-day people, and especially, the narrative pieces young people have voiced and expressed. In discovering the life of these themes around us, we recognize that life itself carries the narrative themes we wish to promote, and thereby we do not have to rely simply on our words to enter into these narratives.

Strategies to See and Give Voice in a Narrative Approach

Given that we possess an abundance of resources that can provide examples, we can insert these narrative examples on every wall, on every screen, and in every ministerial offering. Ultimately, this is how *we* give voice to salvific narratives and themes, and how *we* draw attention to their connection to the lives of young people.

Fundamentally, the more our young people *see it elsewhere*, the easier it will be for them to see it in their own lives. As this connection grows, a comfort zone is created for young people to express their experiences, and pathways are built for them to link their lives to larger salvific narratives and the life of the faith community.

NAMING

An effective approach to the strategy to give voice is *naming*.[7] *Naming* involves the moments, activities, and projects that inspire and challenge young people to name, in small pieces, aspects of their lives related to themes, issues, salvific narratives, questions, and the examples we present.

Importantly, naming includes activities that allow young people to communicate using art forms and expressions. By using creative forms of expression, especially forms they value and utilize, young people are more apt to be engaged, interested, and expressive. Conversely, they are often reluctant to speak their feelings or verbalize their pains that long to be healed. Thus, by introducing other ways to express experiences and longings, young people are afforded a chance to express pieces of their lives in a variety of unique ways.

These ways may include writing, physical action, artwork, acting, small-group sharing, and others that we discuss later. One simple form is the use of a make-shift chalkboard that we repeatedly inserted along the path of obstacle courses, in the middle of constructed rituals, and as part of biblical reenactments and prayer experiences. I'm always amazed at what our young people write in response to tag lines, such as, "Write your pains here," "What do you fear?" and "What's the best thing about home?"

As a process, *naming* involves personal reflection and private moments to ponder, write, and/or create, but then *naming* also involves sharing, performing, or displaying (if it is a creative project) in public space. The movement from personal to communal space is important to the salvific nature of giving voice, and *naming* helps this movement happen. We must, therefore, take great care to value each expression and utterance, and provide affirming avenues for young people to name and breathe out loud in communal space.

To further assist this effort to name and give voice always and everywhere, the following *naming* categories may inspire moments, activities, and projects in which we ask our young people to

Write it!

Journaling, letter writing, storytelling, statements, word art, chalkboard writing, screenwriting, poetry, short stories, continuing the sentence, and the like

Say it!

Testimonies, storytelling, small group sharing, verbal prayer, confession, checking-in sessions, yelling, poetry, and the like

Sing it!

Musical performance, talent show, liturgical choir, song writing, music recording, and the like

Create it!

Art projects, storyboard drawings, clay work, murals, painting, graffiti, mask making, film production, word art, performance pieces, set design, image projects using smart phones, and the like

Act it!

(includes physical action and performance)

Physical challenges in obstacle courses, walking in processions, trust walks, games, theater games, skits, role-playing, *dinámicas* (interactive group activities/

games with deep meaning), drama, dance, act out what they learned, the use of theater exercises, and the like

Feel it!

Creating prayer and ritual experiences using the senses, music, images, symbols, prayers, readings, and so on that prompt an expressive response

Share it!

Sharing favorite songs (youth sharing their favorite song and the favorite song of their parents and grandparents), bringing symbols from home, sharing writing/art they created, sharing food, and so on

Celebrate it!

Celebrating whenever possible: piñata, play, fun, games, food, food, and food

Strategy #5: Convert Statements into Questions

Certainly, questions are central to the ways in which we engage one another, ponder, reflect, and deepen our understanding. Yet when it comes to young people, too often we jump to making statements about who they are and what they believe rather than considering the value in asking questions. This strategy, therefore, implores pastoral leaders to resist the temptation to overgeneralize and, instead, ask questions, especially *to see* and *give voice* to the unique lives of the youth in our communities.

The strategy to *convert statements into questions* holds a duel-benefit, first, in forcing pastoral leaders to acknowledge the flaws in *our* perceptions. We all carry prejudices and agendas that lead us to make broad statements that often serve to discount the complexity of young people's lives. Our biases also lead us to assume that elements like faith and religion are not important to young people, since they may not express these elements in the same way as older generations. Such misperceptions lead us to make unfair, uniformed statements over what we think young people lack, what we think they need, what we think they should value, and how we think they should act.

Statements such as "Young people today have lost their faith," "Today's youth only care about themselves," "Today's youth have no respect for tradition, or culture, or religion," and "Young people need to put away their phones and learn how to interact with people" can be converted into fruitful questions: "How do young people express their longing for God and love?" "What do they value and why?" "How are cultural and religious symbols, values, and expressions evident in the context of their lives today?" and "How do they interact with others and find meaning in those interactions?"

By converting statements into questions, we generate a curiosity and compassion for salvific narratives, compelling us to enter into their lives and engage them as unique persons. Through such engagements, and by asking questions, we empower our young people to respond through *their* statements, self-expressions, and reflections based on *their* experiences, feelings, and opinions.

Importantly, while their responses are vital, we should not expect young people to provide well-developed verbal responses just as much as we cannot expect that from adults, especially with questions related to faith, well-being, and the development of one's communal identity. As such, our converted questions are best viewed as part of our overall strategies *to see* and *give voice*, which means we need to use a variety of strategies and approaches and utilize a variety of artistic forms for young people to give voice to the realities related to the questions we convert from our statements.

Strategy #6: Name the Salvific Themes We See

So far, we have explored strategies invested in seeing, giving voice, and creating ways in which young people tell us who they are. While this investment is ongoing, the strategy to *name salvific themes* focuses on *our* ability to express and give meaning to the narrative themes we see, hear, and intuit, knowing that all narrative pieces carry salvific potential.

Starting with the experiences youth *give voice* to and the daily-life expressions and realities we *see*, we gain insights into the themes at work, the salvific themes that connote a participation in relationships, and unveil the challenges that hinder those relationships. Through careful reflection and dialogue, these insights help us to identify the themes that emerge from their relational experiences, expressions, and disconnections, but that also point to something more, to a deeper longing and a larger salvific whole. Such familiar salvific themes include forgiveness, friendship, grief, prayer, birth, death, food, family, well-being, and justice.

In naming these themes, we must also recognize the salvific nature in themes associated with human struggles and experiences of alienation: themes such as isolation, addiction, mental illness, heartache, discrimination, violence, self-hatred, aggression, and street life. Here, we are reminded of the God in Genesis moving humanity toward each other, searching for us when we hide, and making clothes when we experience shame and nakedness.

We, too, must step into this beautiful salvific dynamic by first recognizing that these painful experiences are not final, but are experiences that long for healing, reconciliation, communion, and relief. As such, they are salvific themes in need of our accompaniment toward salvific wholeness. By naming themes in this manner, we participate in giving voice to the salvific nature revealed and hidden in all dimensions of the lives of young people. We also inspire our capacity to build upon and utilize these themes in connecting their lives to others.

Notably, in doing the work of *naming*, we must know that salvific themes are often hidden in expressions and realities we do not see, do not value, or do not understand. As in the case of *cariño*-fighting, I did not expect to *see* it, nor did I immediately name it as a salvific expression. By entering into dialogue, however, I heard from the youth of the community that it carried salvific meaning—"out of *cariño.*" This still did not cause me to name

117

cariño-fighting as a salvific theme, but it did move me to recognize it as an expression that carries salvific meaning, which then caused me to begin the process of naming the salvific themes linked to the expression of *cariño*-fighting.

This effort *to see* and *give voice* to the narratives connected to *cariño*-fighting led me to see and name a host of salvific themes linked to narratives in the daily lives of Hispanic youth of Boyle Heights: themes such as bodily identity, kinship, death, initiation, discrimination, Mexican culture, play, street life, shame, hope, violence, *La Virgen*, walking, popular religiosity, and hopelessness. Each of these salvific themes represents both the expressions that brought such themes to our attention and a larger unarticulated salvific whole to which each theme longs to connect.

As a strategy, naming the salvific themes in the lives of young people moves what we *see* into a deeper process of reflection. It causes us to enter more deeply into the narratives to which the themes point so that we can appreciate the fullness of each narrative and facilitate its ability to transform both the individual and the community.

Consequently, by naming salvific themes based on real human struggles and joys, we generate narrative connections between young people and the people that surround them (family, older generations, and the faith community). This enables rich dialogue and engagement based on shared and unique themes. By interweaving lives in this way, we can continue the narratives of young people from within a wider relational embrace, which ultimately brings to life the salvific healing and communion they long to experience. We now move to the next set of strategies that are designed to explore how we can facilitate this interweaving of lives.

9

Bringing Narratives Together by Bringing Lives Together

I suffer from depression and panic disorder. It is in my genes and can be traced back to my grandmother and was passed on to my mother, my aunt, uncles, brothers, sisters, cousins, nephews, nieces, my son, and me. It is a painful disease that shows up with certain triggers but also shows up unexpectedly.

Only recently has my family given voice to our mental illnesses, shedding light on our family history and empowering us to walk with each other in our pain. Before that, we each dealt with it in isolation—many of us not even knowing how to define it. Still suffering, we look for ways together to manage the dark times and thrive as we embrace this part of our identity.

In hope, I created a panic kit for my son, which was as much a symbolic gesture as it was practical. It included a crying towel, homeopathic medicines, scripture readings, toys, pictures, books, and an icon with the inscription, "Come to me, all you who are weary and burdened, and I will give you rest."

Still, we suffer. So we created a WhatsApp group called *Family Support*, and while we often use it to casually interact, its purpose is to have a space for us to say, "Help! I hurt!" In those times, we can instantly rush to each other's side and be together (cyberly speaking). In this space, we can provide comfort and encourage deeper investments into the physical, psychological, and spiritual ways to bring about relief.

This narrative of my life perfectly illustrates the heart of this chapter—*bringing narratives together by bringing lives together*. By applying a narrative framework to my experience, I have given voice to a salvific narrative fragment hidden throughout most of my life, connected to a history of generations, enabled by a culture of shame and silence, evident in my family way of being, and linked to my physical, psychological, and spiritual composition and well-being.

Yet while these narratives existed in my family for generations, only recently have we brought them to the foreground, uttering our pain out loud in relational space. It wasn't until we gave voice that we started to see the connected and disconnected narratives just mentioned—exposed like a salvific puzzle longing for our separate narratives to be brought together. So, we did. We continued the narratives. We created a village of relationships to be present to each other and to respond to our darkest pains and fears. Although we still suffer, we transformed our fragmented narratives by bringing our lives together and participating together in the salvific nature of our being.

For pastoral leaders, that is what it means to nurture the salvific narratives in the lives of our young people. By connecting lives, we enact our most basic and fruitful function as pastoral leaders. In doing so, we move from the work of *seeing* to the work of *connecting*.

Strategy #7: Participate in Movement and Continue the Narrative

As human beings created to be in relationship, we long to be more; our narrative expressions, pieces, and fragments long to be connected to larger life-giving narratives. Thus far, we have illustrated this fundamental claim by joining together narratives and theological concepts to understand and recognize this salvific process imbued in each person. Consequently, two central themes emerge as strategies for pastoral leaders. They are *participating in movement* and *continuing the narrative.*

PARTICIPATING IN MOVEMENT

In our discussion of the Genesis Creation/fall story in chapter 3, we proposed that a basic human *movement* exists—from *aloneness* to relationality—animated by God and made real by the people that surround us. *Movement* best describes this salvific dynamic since it spotlights the ultimate purpose of life—to be in relationship—and gives value to the human experience of alienation from which we are pulled outward into relational space. Movement, in this way, captures the form and function of our salvific nature by describing both the human dance within this dynamic and God's unending movement of all creation toward God's loving embrace.

From within this paradigm, we recognize the significance in the small expressions and grand utterances that move our longings and sufferings into relational space. We also come to know that in movement we are not alone, since *movement*, by definition, is a relational endeavor requiring the presence of others with us.

In fact, pastoral leaders participate in *movement* by continuing the narratives we see in the lives of our young people. By continuing the life of the narratives in the daily lives of young people, such as those illustrated in part 2, we, in effect, help to enliven and sustain the relationality longed for in their narratives, and we become a viable resource, inviting others to join in their journey toward joyful communion and wholeness.

As illustrated in my mental health narrative, the movement from isolation to family accompaniment involved much of the salvific strategies already proposed, but it also included our responsibility to continue our narratives together. The desire to step toward wholeness compelled us to remain attentive to our suffering narratives while also drawing from family love and our village of relationships—friends, therapists, doctors, and spiritual guides. The collective attention on our mental anguish inspired us to imagine what healing, relief, and wholeness might look like, which led us to consider all the narratives and people needed for this to happen.

This illustration captures what it means to *continue the narratives* and *participate in the movements* of young people, and pinpoints several key elements that require further attention to engage both as ministerial strategies. These elements are "Narratives Continue," "Imagining the *More*," and "Bringing Lives Together."

NARRATIVES CONTINUE

The narratives pastoral leaders encounter in the lives of young people are typically glimpses of narratives that continue in fruitful and painful ways, requiring pastoral leaders not only to see the glimpses but also to pay attention to how they are continued and expressed.

For example, in many ways young people are continuing their narratives toward healing and reconciliation as they participate in twelve-step programs, faith formation, addiction recovery, healthy living, grief work, the sacrament of reconciliation, therapy, and the like. They are also contributing to the wholeness of their peers and community as they tend to the needs of friends, family members, and the neighborhood, witnessed in the care of peers demonstrated by the music camp youth discussed in chapter 4.

The narratives of young people also continue in harmful ways and into deeper experiences of anguish and isolation. We often see signs of these moments in their eyes, in their silence, and by their absence. As narratives continue in these ways, the possibility of harm and suffering increases. For that reason alone, we must do all we can to uncover the experiences of alienation and assist in bringing the person into relational space.

As narratives continue into relationality, the possibility of healing, wholeness, and salvific communion are made real. This is not to say that aloneness and relationality don't exist simultaneously or that degrees of each are not happening. Yes, there is a complexity that we may never uncover. However, there is also a simplicity to the salvific nature of our being, which we must convert into a fundamental function of ministry. In other words, pastoral leaders must participate in the continuation of narratives by bringing lives together to (a) sustain the beauty of the life-giving relationships in the lives of young people and (b) hold their suffering and alienating narratives in relational space. In this way, we point to the *more* that each narrative seeks.

IMAGINING THE *MORE*

Like the notion of *movement*, famed theologian Karl Rahner asserts his belief that God continually beckons the person toward something more. In presenting Rahner's work, Geffrey Kelly writes, "God is ever present in enhancing one's freedom, uplifting consciousness, and providing the awe, unrest, questioning, and movements of love that lead to a deepening of one's experience of both God and self."[1] Wrapped within this proclamation, Rahner reveals a God committed to the fullness of our being, drawing us deeper into who we are through the many salvific elements highlighted in this narrative approach. Central to this salvific movement is the imagination—the spark that invites us to dream of something life-giving that is both who we are and intimately connected to something more.

In general, we know that *more* means relationality, communion, wholeness, and healing. In concrete terms, each narrative reveals a longing that "leads to a deepening of one's experience of both God and self." As a strategy, we are therefore called to step into narratives in search of the *more* revealed in its expressions and utterances. As we do that, we can assist in continuing the narrative by imaging what the *more* looks like.

For example, the story of Jesus walking on the water (see Matt 14:22–33) reveals a series of movements that, in turn, reveal insights into what Peter and the others long to experience. The story moves:

> From fear of the storm (and ghost) to "Take heart, it is I; do not be afraid,"
>
> From recognizing Jesus to Peter longing to be closer to Jesus on the water,
>
> From Peter walking on the water to Peter feeling the storm and sinking,

From "Lord, save me!" to "Jesus immediately reached
out his hand and caught him," and

From the chaos of the storm to calm winds.

By stepping into this narrative and identifying the *movement*,
we can see what Peter wants: to not be afraid, to have courage in
his communion with Jesus, to imagine new possibilities in Christ,
to step into his storms, to cry out to Jesus when sinking, to know
that he will be caught, to be at peace. These are but a few desires
we gain by looking closer at the narrative, each requiring further
imagination to know what it means for Peter to not be afraid and
to be in communion with Christ.

Similarly, recalling the encounters between the youth in
Boyle Heights and college students, we heard in their voices and
saw in their expressions the movements they imagined and longed
to make real:

From violence to safety,

From fear in isolation to fun and laughter in
community,

From silence to empowerment in public speaking,

From the challenges of street life to the naming of their
dreams and passions, and

From a fond memory to the imagining of a haunted
house.

In relational space, they imagined something more for the
children in their community, something they could make real
for them. So, they did. They created a haunted house in a violent
neighborhood on Halloween night, bringing together the people
of the community in full support.

In both examples, we *see* how the movements in the narratives reveal suffering, longing, and hope. By naming these movements, pastoral leaders uncover what our young people imagine,
and, in doing so, the longing they express moves into our space,
into our imagination gifted to us by God. Empowered by God,
we can then participate in the imagining of *more* and imagine the

specific village of relationships needed in order to bring it to life. As that happens, our young people experience what it means to be surrounded by the love and care of the community.

Bringing Lives Together

By *continuing* the narratives of young people and by imagining the *more* in which they long for, we inevitably come to imagine the people involved and needed to make it real. For example, the longing for the Hispanic youth in Boyle Heights to create a haunted house required the involvement of the entire community, including the parish leadership team, the neighborhood parents, store owners, Homeboy Silkscreen, Proyecto Pastoral, the men at the Guadalupe Homeless Program, law enforcement, the families of the youth involved, the ongoing persistence of the young people in creating a fun and scary haunted house, and my personal accompaniment.

This example serves to demonstrate *our* movement, as pastoral leaders, in finding the people in the community with the heart, ability, and time to contribute to the well-being of our young people in a very specific way. Our task, then, is to enter a relationship with the family and community members that can walk with our young people in their longing for recovery, joy, wellness, and love. Still, our imagination does not end there; for we are continually called to imagine creative ways to sustain these lives together and facilitate new transformative narratives. Consequently, we, too, are enlivened by entering a salvific process linked to *our* more, our longing to apply our gifts and contribute to the transformation of our young ones.

Strategy #8: Foreground the Hidden Narratives

In foregrounding, we come to recognize the overlapping nature of these strategies as they connect to each other and interweave to function within an overall narrative approach. Foregrounding is presented as a separate strategy to emphasize the need for pastoral leaders to remain attentive to those who remain hidden and to what we don't see. As such, this strategy focuses on the needs of young people on the peripheries.

The term *foregrounding* is a concept associated with Alejandro García-Rivera, who describes it as "the lifting up of a piece of background and, then, giving it value, therefore 'foregrounding' it."[2] For García-Rivera, foregrounding is embodied in the biblical principle "lifting up the lowly," proclaimed in Mary's Magnificat (see Luke 1:46–55) and witnessed in Jesus's lifting of the outcast, infirmed, and oppressed.[3] As an act that "lifts up the lowly," foregrounding is an act that makes real the ongoing presence of the risen Christ in the midst of human darkness and pain. Therefore, foregrounding has an incarnational and salvific quality: "It implies that all human 'foregroundings' are, in a sense, an image of the incarnation, and as such possess a redemptive character."[4]

While there are many ways in which foregrounding takes place to the benefit of young people, two specific areas of emphasis contribute to its viability as a strategy for ministry: "Name and Respond to What Is Hidden" and "Foreground Broken Social Systems."

NAME AND RESPOND TO WHAT IS HIDDEN

As a strategy, foregrounding challenges us to give attention to what's hidden in the background, who is cast aside, who is invisible and uncared for, and who is not a part of or feels excluded from the faith community. By shifting our location and investing in young people living on the literal and metaphoric edges of society, we can *see* pains, struggles, and issues that hide in the shadows of their lives. In these instances, we benefit from the power of giving voice and naming to compassionately tend to our youth who are suffering.

As examples, I recall driving to McDonald's one day with a young person, who turned to me and asked, "Is it OK to hate my father?" On a different occasion, a young man told me, "I think I have depression." Then there was the time when a youth asked me what it was like when my high school was on lockdown. There was also the time when the three girls expressed their grief over their friend who had committed suicide, and the time when I could see the fear in a young man's eyes when he told me that he was undocumented. Finally, there was the young woman who informed me that she had to sleep in her car.

Each of these moments appeared in an instant, revealing pains, issues, and societal failings brought to light through their utterances voiced *in the relational space between us.* In each instance, we—the faith community—were challenged to respond through continual presence and ongoing accompaniment of their painful narratives, which we did. Yet, in truth, we could have done more. We can always do more, which is a feeling that represents the imperfect nature of foregrounding: feeling like we are dropping the ball, or not having enough time or resources. However, in the brave utterances of their pain, transformation began and continued with our commitment to remain present.

As part of the strategy to name what is hidden, storytelling emerges as a viable tool that helps generate discussions around painful themes. Stories from Scripture, movies, books, YouTube, and so on, allow young people to *see* issues and realities in the lives of the characters of the story. This, in turn, creates opportunities for young people to express similar issues in their own lives.

For example, I recall foregrounding perceptions of beauty during a confirmation session only to have a young girl later reveal that she struggles with anorexia. In that moment, she bravely gave voice to her suffering, which prompted us to respond with compassion, ongoing accompaniment, parental involvement, and resources for therapy and health care.

In another example, by performing the story of the Woman Accused (see John 8:1–11), the issue of bullying arose and became a central theme as personal stories and concerns were voiced. In response, a second version of the biblical story was created to foreground cyberbullying and highlight the ways in which, like Christ, we are called to be present and affirm the sacred value of the person.

Other examples of things hidden include immigration issues, violence, homelessness, eating disorders, mental illness, suicide, stress, gang life, poverty, poor health, addiction, hunger, police abuse, prejudice, family issues, social injustices, and so on. As we name and give voice to these experiences, we imagine what is needed to bring about healing and wholeness; we continue the narratives by bringing forth a village of relationships—including involvement from local social service agencies and community organizations—needed to care for the well-being of each individual young person, as well as respond to issues at systemic and institutional levels.

By creating space to give voice or by recognizing that which is not voiced, we carry the burdens of young people with them as Jesus does with us. In doing so with the utmost care, we bring these sufferings into a communal space—into the Body of Christ. By inviting community members to pray, and by drawing on local professionals and community resources, the community can walk with young people to bring healing and hope and face injustices.

Foreground Broken Social Systems

As we foreground the hidden and invisible narratives, we confront social and political systems that are broken and persist in persecuting, ignoring, and/or demonizing our Hispanic young people, their families, and the communities in which they live. Therefore, foregrounding raises awareness around the social systems, practices, and attitudes needing reform.

Foregrounding sheds light on systems such as immigration, which perpetuates the separation of families, the fear of deportation, and the underlined racist and discriminatory themes that drive the current laws. Such foregrounding, in turn, inspires communities to organize and push for new policies and reform, and to create safety nets, responses to ICE raids, communal prayer services, and networks of people, lawyers, and advocacy organizations.

As another example, in response to neighborhood violence, the Dolores Mission community created a Safe Passage Program designed to ensure safety for the children walking to and from school each day. The program involves community volunteers standing on street corners while children are en route, creating a link of adults stretching from street to street. Safe Passage also includes designated homes recognized by the children as safe havens should violence erupt in the streets.

In another instance, Dolores Mission, in response to the flawed healthcare system, arranged for mobile dental units to come to the church parking lot and provide dental care for the neighborhood youth and families. In yet another example, in response to the overcrowded educational system, the community established one-on-one tutoring for middle school and high school students and those wanting to get their GED.

Political responses are also required as social needs persist, prompting community involvement through contacting politicians, organizing marches and rallies, participating in social movements, and attending town hall meetings to voice concerns and promote the care of our young people left isolated and vulnerable.

Through foregrounding, we highlight the most painful sufferings of young people by stepping into the dark hidden spaces and alleys that reveal those left alone in pain, calling us to raise a village of relationships to be present and respond as the Body of Christ. Of course, this happens at all levels and involves personal care, the attention of local social services and agencies, and communal efforts to change social structures and attitudes.

Essentially, the young people we encounter are an integral part of the Body of Christ and are empowered to contribute as leaders to the healing aspired by all. Young people must, therefore, be invited into the foregrounding process and considered primary contributors to the village of relationships that accompany and continue to give voice to the pains of our invisible youth. Above all, this bond in kinship is our most precious protection against the forces and pains endured by our young people, their families, and our communities.

Strategy #9: Dialogue between Generations

Bringing lives together centers on our efforts to remain present to our young people and to enliven their fullness of life. In doing so, we embolden their capacity to bring new life to the

entire community and affirm the diversity of peoples and generations that make up our vibrant neighborhoods. In bringing lives
together, we also recognize that our ministerial efforts cannot
simply focus on the narratives of young people but must include
all surrounding narratives since they interact and weave together,
bringing new meaning to both the lives of young people and who
we are as diverse communities. Specifically, it is the multigen-
erational reality alive in each community that contributes to the
identities of young people, their families, and the communities in
which we live.

In emphasizing generations, we acknowledge the primacy
of family, community, and history, all of which are central to the
overall identity of Hispanic peoples and must be viewed through
the unique lens of each generation. This emphasis addresses, in
part, our inability to understand the meanings behind distinctions
between generations and our failure to promote generational
diversity in what it means to be Hispanic. Such failure creates isolation, identity confusion, and feelings of rejection among many
of today's Hispanic young people.

As a ministerial strategy, therefore, we can facilitate intergenerational dialogues, involving family and community members, as a means for each generation to (a) foreground its unique
cultural-religious identity; (b) connect the generations by recognizing similarities in salvific themes (although often expressed
differently); (c) present challenges to each other; and (d) promote
growth, understanding, and further interactive engagements.

Consequently, as a strategy, two central themes stand out that
assist our efforts to facilitate dialogues between generations practically and effectively. They are "Dialogue Using Identity Questions"
and "Dialogue Using Salvific Themes."

DIALOGUE USING IDENTITY QUESTIONS

In the fifth strategy, "Convert Statements into Questions," we
presented several statements that older generations have directed
toward younger ones, indicating a lack of understanding by older
generations as to the meaning and life-giving nature of expressions and relational forms. Of course, the opposite is also true, as

younger generations often misunderstand and challenge the identity expressions of older generations. In response, a positive and effectual dialogue may ensue by converting statements on generations into questions.

Centering on questions related to identity, specifically its relational, cultural, and religious dimensions, benefits the dialogue between generations. While the range of questions may vary, there are several standard identity questions designed to initiate rich conversations and lead to other appealing questions. These include the following: Where do you come from? Who are you? Who is your God? What are your dreams? The beauty of these questions is that they naturally lead to stories related to migration, border crossings, family members, romance, food, culture, traditions, sacred religious expressions, language, cultural loss, God, *La Virgen*, dreams, hopes, and fears.

By exploring identity questions such as these, each generation is able to see the diversity and sameness between generations, resulting in a deeper understanding and value of each other. For example, they may each share their desire for cultural belonging but express their *Latinamente* differently, as younger generations share their unique bilingual/bicultural in-between identity and older generations share stories of living in their country of origin. They may each share their desire for experiences of the Divine, but for younger Hispanic generations, it may involve nontraditional symbolic forms and somatic and relational expressions; while for older generations, it may involve traditional religious symbols, images, and expressions. They may each share their desire for meaningful relationships, but for Hispanic youth, it may include a diversity of self-identities, including LGBTQ youth, as well as a diversity of forms of communication such as those related to social media; while for older generations, it may include traditional ways of being family, involving family responsibility, cultural traditions, and communal celebrations.

By facilitating dialogue around the unique ways of being Hispanic, religious, and relational, the identity of each generation is given a voice. In kind, Hispanic youth enrich their identity as they give voice to it and as it is valued and supported by family and community members. Fundamentally, by engaging Hispanic youth at this level of being, family and community can accompany and foster the growth of Hispanic youth from the inside out. In gaining trust and access to who they are, we can nurture the development of key areas of identity that promote a positive and generative sense of self, community, and faith life.

DIALOGUE USING SALVIFIC THEMES

Drawing on the sixth strategy, "Name the Salvific Themes We See," we find dialogical themes with older generations. Imagine the lively interactions between generations based on experiences of bodily expressions such as tattoos, walking, dancing, friendship encounters, forms of communication, music, forgiveness, death, gang initiation and Christian initiation, discrimination, food and celebration, responsibility to family, culture, shame, violence, hopelessness, and hope.

In facilitating dialogue around these salvific themes, we are prompted to think creatively about how to bring generations together and to allow for the uniqueness and sameness of each to be expressed in the company of other generations. Such ways may include role-playing, naming activities, art projects, liturgical moments, prayer experiences, celebrations, retreat experiences, and, of course, dialogue circles.

The fruitfulness of these endeavors is that, like the identity questions, they naturally lead each generation to step into the lives of others, inspiring generations to remain present to each other and accompany each other. Ultimately, in centering on the salvific themes and the unique cultural-religious identities of generations young and old, new narrative possibilities emerge, ones that are transformative and inclusive of the diversity of people and generations in the community.

10

The Animation of Sacred Space

You may recall from chapter 1 the story of my son's initiation that night at the Mission San Luis Rey Church: how God showed up in the form of a locked museum door, a seven-foot wall, and a pitch-black room. And there we both were—using what we had been given in the sacred space animated by four generations of men, a space stepped into by God.

On that night, *the curtain was torn in two*, revealing a familiar and yet new way of being for us, one in which our familiar existence was awakened by a salvific narrative that had been with us and in us all along but had yet to be exposed. In the communion of these narratives, we were transformed—experiencing God with us, and requiring nothing from us but to live this communion.

Over the years, I have come to trust and rely on the grace-filled spark that happens when narratives are brought together, especially when we animate sacred space by bringing lives together within *the grand narrative*—God's life with us. Here, we encounter the heart of this closing chapter: to enliven transformative narratives and animate sacred space within the life of God.

Confident that transformative narratives happen in the landscape of everyday life, this chapter focuses on our intentional efforts to awaken glimpses of a God who is in love with the young people of your communities. By doing so, we continue to bring young people and their narratives together in sacred—symbolic, communal, ritual—spaces that inspire the utterance of the salvific words "Speak, for your servant is listening" (1 Sam 3:10). Our hope is to shed light on the divine reality already alive with and in the young people of our communities. With that goal, let us now consider the final three strategies for a narrative approach: "Continue the Narratives in Hispanic Catholic Popular Religiosity," "Create Ritual Experiences," and "Inspire Transformative Responses Using Scripture."

Strategy #10: Continue the Narratives in Hispanic Catholic Popular Religiosity

To articulate clearly the potential, utility, and salvific connectivity of this strategy, we must first increase our awareness of the living narratives in Hispanic Catholic popular religiosity and uncover what this means for today's Hispanic young people who are disconnected from them. This dynamic ultimately inspires questions and creative resolutions around how to move forward in animating sacred space for the Hispanic youth in our communities.

THE TRANSFORMATIONAL CHARACTER IN HISPANIC CATHOLIC POPULAR RELIGIOSITY

There is something salvific and necessary within the landscape of Hispanic Catholic popular religiosity—something that pastoral leaders must uncover and hold onto despite its fading influence on many Hispanic young people today. Hopefully, pastoral leaders will *continue this narrative* into the lives of younger Hispanic generations. To do this, we must recognize the transformational character and salvific significance in Hispanic Catholic popular religiosity and bring to the foreground several key features.

First, as discussed in chapter 5, the religiosity of Hispanic peoples, historically, has long served to unite and transform two persistent narratives: the experience of oppression and marginalization, and the longing to experience the Divine. Through affective, bodily, communal, and symbolic interactions, and ritual forms, Hispanic Catholic popular religiosity has brought about a transformational communion between these narrative themes. As previously noted, the passing on of this salvific way is done through such experiences, which the body recognizes as salvific and longs for in each generation—often appearing as new forms of expression.

Second, ritual best describes the way this salvific process emerges. While the concept of ritual is far reaching and beyond what we hope to accomplish in this strategy, it is a recognizable spiritual form that provides a way to understand and animate sacred space for the young people we serve. In general, ritual can be described as the symbolic-communal movements, actions, and interactions intentionally designed to expose and awaken the people of the community to a larger relational reality.

In practical terms, ritual exposes the communion between people and God, but it does so in real time, physical space, and with a community of people. This concise nature of ritual is affirmed by Richard Rohr, who says that if we can "get it" in the condensed moments, then we can see it in the whole of life:

> Good ritual is always somehow about love and death, but in a distilled form and a concise frame. When we "get it" in a confined and compressed space, we can then start seeing the mystery everywhere, and any split between the sacred and the profane eventually breaks down. The temple and church are only to get you started; they are not a place to stay. Temple, church, and mosque should teach you *how* to see, but *what* you need to see is *outside* and *everywhere*.[1]

Third, and in the words of famed ritual scholar Victor Turner, "ritual transforms."[2] Here, Turner proclaims the ultimate function of ritual as a symbolic-communal endeavor designed to transform the people of a community. As part of this function, ritual underscores the historical and generational existence of *intentionality*— the intentionality behind creating, organizing, and participating in ritual encounters in the hope of experiencing a glimpse of the

Divine, of awakening and experiencing a communion of narratives within the life of God.

From a narrative perspective, through ritual, we are reminded of *transformation narratives* filled with intention, hope, human work, and God's grace—alive in the history of Hispanic Catholic popular religiosity and interwoven into the lineage of Hispanic young people. This is relevant for our work with Hispanic youth, since what we often encounter today are fragmented narratives longing for transformational experiences, experiences we recognize in a history of Hispanic religiosity.

Here is where we make the connection between the transformation young people seek and the transformational dimension alive in their cultural-religious history and identity. This connection between young and old cannot be overstated, and we must rejoice in the reality that there is a transformational aspect to Hispanic religiosity connected to the identity of young Hispanics today; a religiosity that tells us how and in what ways we can intentionally animate transformative narratives within the living context of Hispanic young people. In strategic terms, we have a rich treasure (salvific themes, ritual forms, and communal-symbolic actions) to draw from to animate a communion of narratives invested in the lives of our young people.

THE DISCONNECTION BETWEEN GENERATIONS

Defined as the religiosity of the people, Hispanic popular religion lives on in families, homes, and in faith communities across the United States. The salvific life embodied in the myriad of traditions continues to wash over and transform the life of many Hispanic generations today. Yet, for many young Hispanics, the disconnection with this long-standing narrative is equally palpable, especially for 1.5-, second-, and third-generation Hispanics and beyond.

Many young Hispanics today, through no fault of their own, find themselves isolated from a symbolic-spiritual-communal network that *intentionally* provides moments, encounters, and processes designed to hold the fullness of their lives within the life of God. While we recognize this reality in the history of Hispanic popular religiosity, many Hispanic young people do not experience this overarching spirituality today.

Thus, while the salvific nature alive in each young person persists in finding ways to experience God's love and salvific meaning, and, moreover, while the life of God unceasingly lures each young person into God's embrace, there is an underlying lack of intentionality, a lack of something purposefully designed by faith communities that involves the daily existence of young people and seeks to interweave that existence with glimpses of God's love. Strategically, this brings us back to ritual and the animation of sacred space.

Overall, we are reminded of Eli, who enlivened Samuel's encounter with God by placing what Samuel was already hearing within sacred space—within the context of the dynamic between Samuel and God—leading Samuel to recognize God in his own life and step deeper into that life as a result. Similarly, we, too, are called to enact that level of intentionality by purposefully providing ritual experiences, encounters, and processes designed to hold the fullness of young people's lives within the life of God.

Here, we must avoid a cut-and-paste mentality. For while our ability to duplicate powerful cultural-religious traditions is good, as is our capacity to invite our young people to all that our faith communities offer, we cannot rely solely on these to bring about a communion with them and to affect the transformation they seek.

Given that the life of God persists in the everyday lives of young people and knowing that within these "narratives," God is revealed to them—we must build upon this rich soil; we must refashion something old into something reshaped and new for it to matter to them, for it to make sense to them, and for it to hold their individual lives within a larger communal whole.

CONTINUING THE NARRATIVES

As the central aim of this strategy, pastoral leaders must initiate a movement, a continuation of something old into the creation of something new, involving the animation of rituals, prayers, and experiences that hold both old and new together. In doing this, new challenges arise regarding *how* we are to accomplish this work, assuming we are convinced *why* it is needed. The first step in this strategy is to identify the narrative themes and ritual forms alive in Hispanic popular religiosity. Such forms and themes represent the ways in which Hispanic popular religiosity can influence and be integrated into the construction of salvific and transformative communal-ritual spaces designed to integrate the lives of young Hispanics today. Here is a list that outlines Hispanic Catholic popular religiosity, which will prove fruitful as we consider the final strategies specifically designed to create these sacred spaces.

Hispanic Catholic popular religiosity can be described as

Communal: It is a relational endeavor embodied by family, the faith community, generations, and daily life.

Cultural: It lives within a larger cultural-communal network connected to history, country, traditions and values, and community life.

Deriving from experiences of oppression: It foregrounds the daily life experiences of exile and pain, in history and now.

Building on sacred narratives: It reveres and proclaims sacred narratives such as the Paschal Mystery in the life of Christ encountered in the gospel narratives, the salvific encounter with *La Virgen* alive in the Guadalupe narratives, the lives of the saints and ancestors, and the lives of the people.

Paradoxical: It is not afraid to hold opposites and paradoxes like death/new life, oppression/ salvation, isolation/relationality, sacred/profane, private/public, specific realities/universal truths, and life of the people/life of God.

Exposing God's love: It is intended to expose the people to God's love and animate a transformative experience of God's accompaniment in the totality of life.

Expanding sacred space: It expands the locations of the sacred beyond church boundaries to include the home, family, the streets, public space, daily life, and our communion with the dead.

Being interwoven into the liturgical calendar: It is deeply connected to the liturgical calendar including Advent, Christmas, Ash Wednesday, Lent, Good Friday, Easter Sunday, Pentecost, All Souls' Day, feast days, and holy days.

Highly symbolic and experiential: It comes alive in dance, music, art, song, crucifixes, banners, images, statues, and food.

Bodily: Beyond words it is a bodily endeavor inspiring walking, kissing, hugging, bowing, dancing, eating, movement, singing, smiles, and laughter.

Inspiring a response: It inspires expressions, utterances, and actions that indicate a movement into deeper communion with the life of God, the community, and the self.

Cross-generational: It involves generations alive in family, the neighborhood, and history.

Empowering the freedom to include new realities: It is a living narrative invested in the ongoing life of the people that includes new realities, new contexts, challenges, new encounters, and new ways of being relational.

Trusting that God is always present: It trusts that in the animation of sacred space invested in bringing lives together, God's outpouring of love will be made known.

By naming these salvific themes and ritual forms, our capacity to animate similar sacred spaces is emboldened. Through the efforts of our communities, the traditional salvific life of a people continues in renewed forms and new experiences, as we seek to build on the living contexts experienced by today's young Hispanics. As we move to the remaining strategies, we will consider the practical elements involved in these efforts.

Strategy #11: Create Ritual Experiences

Sacred space is everywhere God lives. As *imago Dei*, we can also say that sacred space is everywhere humanity resides, in fact, it is everywhere creation exists. In this, we encounter the mystery of God not as unknowable but as infinitely manifest and endlessly present. Richard Rohr tells us that God as mystery is characterized "not as an unsolvable problem but as inexhaustible truth. Mystery is endlessly understandable."[3] Thus, God's omnipotent depth and breadth is present and to a degree knowable and experienced in countless imaginable and unimaginable ways.

Given this reality, it may be impractical to assume that we can, or need to, animate sacred space since it is everywhere revealed in limitless encounters, experiences, and moments. Yet, we are counting on this inexhaustible truth. Since God is alive in the totality of our lives, and since sacred space describes that space where creation and Creator inhabit, we merely need to step into the sacred spaces that already exist and, if needed, animate them by turning up the volume.

Several months ago, I attended my granduncle Sotero's funeral. In the family gatherings that preceded the burial rite, many wonderful stories were shared, including how he met his wife, his love for family, his love for baseball, and his dedication to the small printshop he owned. One prominent narrative theme was related to his pride and honor in serving in the military during World War II. In fact, he always wore his veteran hat, which earned him free coffee and much gratitude everywhere he went.

Surrounding the coffin at the burial site, we huddled together as the priest read from Scripture and said some tender words. As this happened, we all stood somewhat silent, privately mourning. Heads bowed in the bright sunlight, we heard a car door slam and turned around to see two fully dressed military officers walking in stride toward us. Standing near the coffin, in total silence one opened his case, raised a trumpet to his lips and blew "Taps."

The note that broke the silence was breathtaking. It awoke something inside all of us, transforming our private mourning into communal weeping. In fact, it gave us permission to do what our bodies longed to do, namely, express our pain in communal space and allow ourselves to be covered in the ritual of the funeral rite.

The military officers continued their ritual by draping the coffin with the American flag followed by the rite of committal. This communion of rites brought together a host of salvific narratives, including church life and military life, a crucifix and a flag (both given to the family), the human reality of life and death, and the narratives of Sotero's life—family, love, and military service.

My granduncle's story represents universal salvific realities coming alive in physical space, a concise space filled with dirt, tears, death, tight embraces, physical anguish, laughter, and movements—all permeated by the angelic sound of a single trumpet.

Similarly, our role in animating sacred space is to ensure that the trumpet is heard in human space and time, reverberating out to all the spaces our young people inhabit. Here, we move to the intentional proclamation of God alive in our young people by calling out, "God's here! God's here! God's here!" By doing this from within their context, what they hear becomes their own genuine transformational encounter and experience, awakening their own unique relationship with God, inspiring their own response, in their own time.

Over the years, I have worked hard at creating ritual experiences, seeing it as an art form requiring study, experimentation, courage, and a team filled with creative energy and unique artistic skills. Together we created lasting ritual experiences, and we also created ones that missed the mark. Overall, the ritual experiences that have proven to be most fruitful have been those based on powerful Bible stories, such as *The Boat* ritual described in chapter 1.

The power and beauty of biblical stories is that they want to be more—they want a human partner, and we, too, want to animate this partnership by placing young people into the stories.

In the following strategy, we consider specific biblical stories and outline approaches and helpful practices for creating ritual experiences based on Bible stories. Here, in this strategy, we will concentrate on the groundwork to better understand the how-to dimensions of ritual making by focusing on the following points of emphasis: "What Is Ritual Built Upon?"; "The Role of Physical Movement"; "The Power of Music"; and "The Salvific Themes in Hispanic Popular Religiosity."

WHAT IS RITUAL BUILT UPON?

The work of constructing rituals and experiences for young people involves designing something that takes place in physical space but somehow represents a deep reality. In other words, we convert the spaces in our parish halls, parking lots, and retreat centers into spaces that signify something deeper, salvific, and related to the dynamic between young people and God. Of course, we can all agree that the surface structures we create (built upon deep structures) are imperfect and can never fully embody the salvific realities of life. Given this limitation, our hope in animating sacred space is to turn up the volume so that our young people can experience a glimpse of something deeper—something they can touch, smell, feel, and encounter.

Fundamentally, the deep reality on which we set out to build experiences is the everyday lives of the young people in our communities. Here is where we benefit from the work of seeing, giving voice, naming, foregrounding, and bringing lives together. Each strategy is designed to reveal narratives and salvific themes, which we can draw from and insert into the ritual experiences we create. From bullying, to kinship, to street life, and to the longing to encounter something more, each can be brought to life in the sacred spaces we animate by interweaving these narrative themes with the narratives of God's life with them.

Strategically, this means that we must also draw from deep structures that uniquely represent God's life with us. As previously noted, biblical stories are ready-made for this work, since they are the Word of God filled with transformational encounters with the Divine.

Our Catholic faith also possesses an abundance of salvific expressions longing to be connected to the lives of young people. Consider the sacraments, the liturgical seasons, saints and feast days, prayer traditions, and spiritual traditions, to name just a few. By identifying shared themes within these treasures, we grow in our efforts to interweave the lives of young people with the life of the local faith community and universal Church. Themes such as eating at table, love, thanksgiving, death, birth, new life in Christ, social justice, initiation, the Communion of Saints, celebration, grief, repentance and many more signify the powerful thematic bond shared between young people and Christian faith life. By building upon such themes and by bringing the sacraments and the liturgical and spiritual life of the community into the sacred spaces we animate, the powerful bond they share will be awakened and allowed to flourish and grow.

THE ROLE OF PHYSICAL MOVEMENT

Bodily actions and the use of bodily senses are key elements in the creation of ritual experiences. Fundamentally, physical movement embodies the transformational essence in the ritual process since it involves bodily expressions that move the person from internal private space to outward relational interaction. In this, we are reminded of the body's ability to know, remember, long for, and seek relational engagements that carry salvific meaning.

We awaken these realities in ritual by involving physical actions, touch, artistic expression, and the use of the senses as the means for young people to encounter the relational communion intended by ritual experiences. For example, based on the salvific theme *family*, a customary practice in retreat work is to gather love letters written by parents, family members, and loved ones, and present these letters to youth at a special time during a retreat. As symbols of love, these precious letters often awaken a heartfelt communion and reconciliation between teenagers and parents. Unfortunately, in some instances, I have witnessed the distribution of letters with very little fanfare. In such instances, we diminish the value of these letters by failing to build an atmosphere that illuminates the sacredness and intimacy they represent.

I recall building a retreat theme around "Love Is like a Suitcase" where a suitcase appeared throughout the retreat, including a treasure hunt to find the key that opened the suitcase. In the end, the key was found in their hearts, and when we finally opened the suitcase, we uncovered the precious gifts hidden inside—the letters. By creating a physical playful engagement with and curiosity around the suitcase over a prolonged period of time, we animated the sacredness and preciousness of the letters, making sure as they read the letters to hold the sacredness of the moment through music, candles, and silence. We later continued the salvific essence of the letters by providing an opportunity to write back and included their responses in the closing liturgy.

As another example, in talking to several groups of young people for the Identity Project, *border crossing* emerged as a strong salvific theme. We heard several stories about shoes related to crossing the U.S.-Mexico border—losing shoes, finding shoes, wearing the wrong shoes. During the retreat, we created an experiential journey based on border crossing, which we animated by creating a physical journey and by using shoes as one of the symbols. To emphasize the symbolism, we included the topic of shoes in an earlier presentation and used their shoes throughout the created experience (writing on them, removing them, having them reappear), highlighting the support, comfort, and protection we long for and receive from loved ones, especially during times of distress and separation.

On another occasion, based on the paschal mystery, we created a multistage ritual that included birth, the weight of life, God's accompaniment, death, and new life, each representing movements within a larger salvific cycle. We physically embodied birth and new life by using large expandable tunnels (from Toys "R" Us) representing birth canals. Each young person physically crawled through the tunnels, symbolizing the physical struggles and darkness that leads to birth and new life.

From these examples, we can see that physical actions in rituals create moments for young people to respond freely. Within the process, let them decide to stay in one place or go in a different direction, or write/draw whatever they choose, or ride a bike or walk, or punch a bag or sit still. In doing so, we give value to their freedom to respond in ways consistent with who they are, and we animate God's presence alive in their expressions and choices. Furthermore, the interactive physical character of rituals not only captures deep realities but also provides challenging and fun ways to interweave narratives and lives. Ultimately, through physical movement, we create memorable moments that represent the responses life requires (like stepping out of a boat) and invite them to move into those moments in their lives knowing that they are not alone.

THE POWER OF MUSIC

Music can be described as the language of the soul, since it has the power to reach into our depths, activate the imagination, and inspire meaningful responses. Consider the power of movie soundtracks that resonate deep within and carry the human struggle, the love and the jubilation embodied in a story. Surely, *Titanic* (1997) would not have had such a strong emotional impact if the soundtrack was not as sublime.

Music is especially important in carrying the variety of tones and contrasting emotions experienced in the salvific encounters and movements we animate. In fact, music can be considered the primary symbolic form upon which animation occurs. As such, it is important to draw from all the music at our disposal, especially the music connected to the lives of our young people, as in the prayer experience with Fr. Greg and Tupac described in chapter 7. We must also make sure to expand beyond Christian and liturgical music, since nearly all music, like narratives, carries salvific potential. In my ministry, I've used a full range of music from Metallica, to Rihanna, to Mozart. Given its importance, we must dedicate time and resources in using music in the rituals we create, and if possible, create soundtracks that include a variety of music, sound effects, and voice-over.

Ultimately, music carries the deep realities we hope to bring forth in ritual experiences. Like the symbolic life in Hispanic religiosity, by emphasizing music as a primary symbol, we open young people to a symbolic world capable of generating a flash of insight, a glimpse that unites young people with God and one another.

DRAWING FROM SALVIFIC THEMES

In building ritual experiences based on the daily lives of Hispanic young people, we encounter a history of generations that contributes to who they are and how they interact with the world around

145

them. Whether disconnected from this history or not, the salvific themes alive in a culture remain in the bones of young people today.

In the previous strategy, we identified some key salvific themes and ritual elements in Hispanic religiosity that could be used, adapted, and integrated into rituals for young people. This is especially relevant for young Hispanics since we are not only drawing from a history of generations but are connecting them to the salvific realities that contribute to who they are.

Thus far in this strategy, we have already discussed key points of emphasis aligned with Hispanic Catholic popular religiosity, such as the use of sacred narratives (the life of young people, the life of the faith community, and scripture narratives), the emphasis on bodily actions and responses, and the use of music as a primary symbolic form. These are fundamental characteristics of Hispanic religiosity that are fundamental to the animation of new ritual experiences.

Adding to these key points of best practices, the connection between old and new continues. Each practice below draws from salvific themes alive in Hispanic Catholic popular religiosity. To draw attention to this connection, the correlating Hispanic religiosity theme (named in the tenth strategy) is identified within the brackets in italics following each.

- Put God in every room, on every wall, on every path, in every space; foreground God's presence at every turn (voice, sign, person, angels, images, scripture passage). [*Built upon sacred narratives; Intended to provide a glimpse; Highly symbolic and experiential*]
- Consider ways to include parents and family members by including symbols from home, love letters, involvement in the ritual experience, and an invitation to celebrate afterward. [*Communal; Generational*]
- Do not be afraid to foreground issues and pains, but make sure to animate God's loving response through family, scripture, symbols, touch, music, prayers, sacraments, and interaction. [*Emerged out of experiences of oppression; Holds seeming opposites; Empowers the freedom to include new realties; Built upon sacred narratives*]

- Consider all the spaces, rooms, parking lots, trails, and streets available, and use the different spaces/rooms to symbolize different moments, tones, or activities. Each space can be a station or stage in the ongoing experience. [*Expands sacred space; Highly symbolic and experiential*]

- Consider the set design or environment for each space as it relates to the movement, encounter, and/or theme, using props, signs, symbols, music, scent, and live action. How do you want the space to feel? What do you want it to communicate? [*Intended to provide a glimpse; Highly symbolic and experiential*]

- Create moments that require a physical response (writing on chalkboards, artistic activities, climbing, crawling, dancing, playing games, holding hands, riding a bike, carrying something heavy, walking). [*Bodily; Inspires a response; Intended to provide a glimpse*]

- Consider all the senses. Use smells, sounds, tastes, touch, and visuals. [*Bodily; Highly symbolic and experiential*]

- Repeat, Repeat, Reappear: Use themes, words, music, symbols, and actions over and over. Symbols may reappear over time and in transformed states such as rocks converted into an altar. [*Intended to provide a glimpse; Highly symbolic and experiential; Expands sacred space*]

- Use Contrast: dark/light, fast/still, loud/silent, heavy music/serene music. [*Holds seeming opposites*]

- Connect to the sacramental and liturgical life of the faith community by using symbols, expressions, music, teachings, and by inspiring participation. [*Interwoven into the liturgical calendar; Built upon sacred narratives*]

- Create moments of reflection, pauses, and silence so they can be still and reflect. [*Bodily; Intended to provide a glimpse*]

- Finish Strong: Make sure the ending is exciting, active, conclusive, and meaningful. [*Intended to provide a glimpse; Inspires a response*]

- Celebrate! Create ways to celebrate as a community, with family, and with each other. [*Cultural; Communal*]

- Trust that God will show up for them, in their own time, in their own way, and through their unique lives. [*Trust that God is always present*]
- Conclude with an opportunity for the youth to reflect on and share their experience. Do your best not to interpret the experience for them, but allow them to imagine how they can extend the experience into their daily lives. [*Built upon sacred narratives; Intended to provide a glimpse*]

By providing best practices to animate sacred space connected to the salvific themes and ritual elements in Hispanic Catholic popular religiosity, we expand our scope of possibilities, knowing that the considerations offered in this strategy can be used in many effective and powerful ways. To bring this together and in demonstration of the themes and practices highlighted, let us now turn to our final strategy, the powerful use of Bible stories within a narrative approach.

Strategy #12: Inspire Transformative Responses Using Scripture

As you know from the performance of *The Boat* in chapter 1, it was in that space between my eleven-year-old son and me that God showed up as I called my son's name to step out of the boat in faith. It was a glimpse shared between father and son that awakened me to the transformative power of a parent calling out the name of his/her beloved child while enacting the word of God. In this, we see the revelatory nature of Bible stories and their enduring ability to inspire transformative responses.

In the remarkable stories of the Bible, we see someone like us struggling with faith, fear, and brokenness, and we see God's presence amid that struggle. Even better, we not only see *that* God is present in these moments, but also *how* God is present, how God is for us—calling us by name, keeping us from sinking, breaching boundaries, lifting the lowly, searching for us, healing us, and clothing us.

With so much great stuff packed into a biblical story, *the story itself wants to be more.* The story wants to be broken open and entered into. As the word of God, the story wants a human partner who will also open up his/her life and tell his/her story so that both stories can be seen as one story woven together.

As a strategy, opening a biblical story effectively requires that we unpack its images, plot points, encounters, symbols, relevance to youth, and salvific themes and movements. By unpacking the elements of a biblical story, we begin to imagine ways to insert young people into the life of the story and ways to link the salvific themes and movements of the story to their daily life experiences. Imagine an entire retreat based on one biblical story; imagine creating a multistage experience or obstacle course based on a story; imagine performing a story and adding new characters and settings that represent the lives of youth; imagine adding an ending to a story to see what happens to certain characters; imagine taking a powerful symbol from a story, like God making clothes, and recreating that moment, and then having that symbol reappear for an entire year; and imagine if your young people voice a pain in their lives that is also in the story: What do we do with that? How does God/Jesus respond to it in the story? How can we accompany our youth like God/Jesus does in the story? The imaginings are endless.

Over the years, I have had the opportunity to open biblical stories and animate powerful experiences based on the characters, salvific themes, and encounters uncovered in the stories. Some of these stories include the story of Creation and the fall (see Gen 1—3), the story of Jesus and Peter walking on the water (see Matt 14:22–33), the story of Jacob and Esau (see Gen 25:19–34), and the story of the woman accused of adultery (see John 8:1–11). In presenting this strategy, these animated experiences will illustrate the power of the word of God within a narrative approach using the following practical approaches: "Choosing a Biblical Story"; "Opening Biblical Stories"; "Asking Questions and Identifying Elements in the Story"; "Relating the Story to the Lives of Young People"; and "Animating Sacred Space Using Bible Stories."

Choosing a Biblical Story

The most immediate requirement in choosing a biblical story is to remain attentive to the unique daily life narratives of the youth in our communities. As we gather with our teams to discern appropriate Bible stories, it is our responsibility to ensure their lives remain central. This can be achieved by inviting young people to partake in these endeavors as full participants on leadership teams.

We must also acknowledge our inclination to choose Bible verses that are not part of a story but profess moral teachings or statements that represent what we think our young people need. While such verses are important and may be inserted into the larger process, avoid foregoing transformative stories in place of short proclamation statements. Aware of this, the following instructions will help in choosing a transformative Bible story:

- The story must include a character(s) that represents *a person struggling* and/or *seeking something more*, and a character that represents *God's loving response and accompaniment*. For example, in the beautiful story of Jacob and Esau, Jacob represents a broken character overcome by fear yet longing to reconcile with his brother, while Esau represents God's forgiveness and desire to be in communion.
- The story must contain the *movement from some form of human struggle to an encounter that brings about some form of transformation*. For example, the story of the fall moves from feeling naked, ashamed, and hiding to God searching and clothing; the story of the prodigal son moves from eating slop with the pigs to an embrace with the father; the story of Jesus walking on the water moves from fear to walking with Jesus to sinking to being saved.
- The story must contain an *encounter*. Connected to the movement, a transformative story always has a moment in which a physical encounter happens between the struggling character and the God charac-

150

ter. For example, in the story of the woman accused, the woman, amid persecution, encounters Jesus—they have a moment filled with salvific actions and words. On the road to Emmaus, the disciples encounter Jesus in the breaking of the bread. In still another example, the women at the tomb are transformed at the site of the empty tomb and in the encounter with the resurrected Christ: "Jesus met them and said, 'Greetings!' And they came to him, took hold of his feet, and worshiped him" (Matt 28:9).

- The story must have a *transformational ending*. Again, connected to movement and an encounter, the story must possess a *salvific conclusion* that is usually tied to the encounter. For example, the story of Jacob and Esau concludes with a loving embrace and kiss, leading Jacob to make an altar to signify God's presence in that moment. In another example, the paralytic man encounters Jesus and is forgiven and healed, walking out of a crowded house for all to see (see Luke 5:17–26). And again, in Paul's conversion, the scales fall from his eyes and he is baptized (see Acts 9).

- The story must be *relevant and inviting* for young people. In discerning relevance, we benefit from our work in seeing and giving voice to their salvific narratives, which we can then recognize in the plots and themes in the story. For example, I became drawn to the story of Jacob wrestling an angel (see Gen 32:23–33) after I recognized the salvific themes in *cariño*-fighting. In another example, we were able to foreground the theme of fear in the lives of young people by recognizing fear as a persistent theme in the story of Jesus and Peter walking on the water. In another instance, we recognized bullying in the story of the woman who was accused and connected it to the issue of bullying in the lives of young people today. By considering relevant themes as part of our discernment process, we eventually arrive at biblical stories with the potential to weave stories and lives together, connecting young people to the Word of God.

Opening Biblical Stories

After choosing a biblical story, it is time to let the life of the story erupt through its characters, images, and dramatic moments. Through the process of *choosing a biblical story*, we have already begun the work of opening it. To continue opening a story, the following instructions can be used by the leadership team, and they can also be used as an activity for young people to *open biblical stories*. Note that young people should become familiar with a biblical story before they interact with the story in a ritual experience, and they should reflect on how the story continues into their lives, after they have encountered the ritual experience. That said, here are several instructions designed to uncover the salvific moments in biblical stories:

- *List the characters and describe their situation*—describe what they are feeling and what they long for. For example, in the story of Zacchaeus, the tax collector, he climbs a tree to see Jesus (see Luke 19:1–10). What stirred him to act in this way? What did he long for and how did his brokenness/sins contribute to his movement toward Jesus? In the story of the woman who was accused, what did the crowd experience in witnessing the woman's encounter with Jesus? Did they walk away in disgust, or were some also transformed by what they witnessed?
- *List the images evoked by the story*—the striking pictures in your mind inspired by the characters and dramatic moments. For example, imagine the struggle on the face of Zacchaeus as he climbs the tree; imagine Jacob wrestling with an angel all night long; imagine God tenderly weaving clothes for the naked man and woman; imagine Jesus kneeling to engage the woman lovingly in the eye; and imagine him writing in the dirt. What did he write?
- *Identify the plot points*, the moments in the story that move the story along to its completion. There is immense value in simply recalling the story, as a reflective exercise for the leadership team, telling the story in our own words. For example, Jacob cheats

152

Esau out of his inheritance, Esau curses Jacob, Jacob flees, years later God commands Jacob to return home, Jacob fears for his life, Jacob wrestles with an angel all night, in fear Jacob walks toward Esau, Esau runs up to Jacob, Esau embraces and kisses Jacob, Jacob builds an altar. In opening this story and identifying the moments in this story, we were inspired to create a multistage experience (obstacle course) that moved through these plot points.

- *Identify the three-part movement*: before the encounter, the encounter, and after the encounter. The aim here is to identify a before and after, which illuminates how the struggling character moves from pain into salvific healing and communion. For example, in the story of the woman who was accused, the woman enters the scene caught, accused, and forcibly dragged into the public space. Jesus encounters the woman as he twice stoops down to enter an intimate sacred space with the woman. It is as if Jesus whispers in her ear as he writes on the ground. Another layer appears in the story as Jesus encounters her accusers, challenging them to recognize their own sins and brokenness. In the end, the woman gets up and leaves truly free from condemnation, while the crowd walks away.

By opening the three-part movement in the story of the woman accused, our team uncovered the bodily actions, words, and symbols used to illustrate this movement: from condemnation, to stooping down and writing, to standing up and walking away free and reconciled. We also recognized the salvific themes (condemnation, fear, betrayal, bullying, intimacy, acceptance, and forgiveness), which we developed as key dialogical points connecting the story to the lives of young people (used before and after the ritual experience). In naming the three-part movement, we also drew attention to *how* Jesus accepts, forgives, and accompanies the woman, and we used these salvific actions to demonstrate to young people how they can imitate Jesus in their encounters with those condemned. We underscored these actions, which will be described later, by inserting young people into the story, as ones who imitate the salvific actions of Jesus.

ASKING QUESTIONS AND IDENTIFYING ELEMENTS IN THE STORY

Choosing a Biblical Story and *Opening Biblical Stories* are practical approaches for pastoral leaders to (a) imagine the many ways in which powerful biblical stories connect to the lives of young people and (b) begin the process of creating ritual experiences built upon these stories. We now move to questions designed for young people to answer directly so that they can engage in the life of Bible stories and name the elements in the stories related to their own lives. For full effect, these questions may be integrated into the instructions for *Opening Biblical Stories* and be continued into the "what if" set of questions presented later. Also, these sets of questions can be inserted as an activity before, during, or after a ritual enactment of the story. Of course, while engaging these questions, new insights and imaginative ideas will be brought to life by young people, prompting pastoral leaders to invest in what young people voice, and inspiring us to include these ideas in the ritual experiences we create. Here are several sample questions:

- What title would you give the story?
- Name the characters in the story.
- How did the story begin? How did it end? How do you feel about the ending of the story?
- Describe a moment or an image in the story that stands out for you.
- Name the struggles experienced by the main character(s), and write a couple of words that describe the brokenness/longing of the main character(s).
- Describe the encounter between the main character and the divine character.
- Did the main character change? Was he or she transformed? How did that happen?
- Name and describe the actions of the divine character.
- What character do you identify with the most and

154

why? What character do you identify with the least and why?

- How might the character(s) have acted differently?
- Tell us a time when something similar happened to you. How did your story end?

In asking young people these questions, pastoral leaders should take advantage of the previous strategies and utilize a variety of ways for young people to reflect, journal, voice, express artistically, and dialogue based on the questions.

RELATING THE STORY TO THE LIVES OF YOUNG PEOPLE

By inviting young people to enter the story, we are asking them to imagine themselves in the story and to imagine the story as part of their own lives. Hopefully, if young people see the human-Divine dynamic in the story, they can start to see it in their own lives, trusting that God also walks with them. An effective way to connect Bible stories to their lives is to continue the process by asking "what if" questions. To reiterate a key point, "what if" questions are designed to arouse creative insights and imaginative proposals that often prompt our attention, inspiring us to act on them either in the moment or later through adapted performances or ritual experiences. Here are some sample "what if"-type questions:

- What if this story happened today? Where would it take place? How would you, your peers, or your parents react?
- Name some situations today that are like the experiences of the main character.
- What if the mother or father of the main character were in the story? What would she/he say to the main character? How would the main character respond?
- What if you could insert yourself into the story, what would you do or say?
- If you were the divine character in the story, how would you have acted? What would you have said or done?

- How would the divine character in the story respond to you, in your life today?
- How would you want the divine character in the story to respond to you?

As an example of "what if" questions for a specific Bible story, below are questions for the story of the woman who was accused (see John 8:1–11):

- If this happened today, what names would the accused woman be called?
- If you were the parent of the woman, what would you say to her? What would you say to the crowd? What would you say to Jesus?
- How are you alike and/or different from the accusers? Do you accuse yourself or others?
- If you were Jesus, what would you have written in the dirt?
- If you witnessed the encounter between the woman and Jesus, how would you be affected?
- How would you respond to the woman if you encountered her at the end? What would that look like?
- What are your peers being accused of today?
- What would Jesus write in the dirt for your peers?
- Imagine the next day for the woman. What is she thinking, feeling, and doing?
- If it were you, what would your next day be like?
- Imagine the next day for the people in the crowd.
- Imagine the next day for Jesus.

By imaging the life of the story as part of the lives of young people, "what if" questions create ideas wherein the salvific nature of the story is imagined in new ways. Imagine young people writing scripts, taking on new roles, and rehearsing and performing a readapted Bible story. Imagine a performance that stops for reflection and then continues with new spontaneous characters or new lines for the characters. Imagine continuing the story by adding "the next day" for the main characters. Imagine expanding the

156

sacred space of the story by performing it in the streets, at the local park, in the parish hall, during a homily, or as part of a street procession. These are but a few of a multitude of ways in which the life of the story continues into the lives of our young people.

ANIMATING SACRED SPACE USING BIBLE STORIES

By entering into Sacred Scripture, we have enacted the salvific intent of biblical narratives—the intent to be opened, encountered, and continued into everyday life. Throughout this strategy, we have participated in this intent by considering ways and asking questions designed to expose and awaken the salvific essence alive in the communion between young people and the word of God. In this last section, we continue this intent by returning to the notion of animating sacred space.

By creating ritual experiences built upon biblical stories, our aim is to open these stories in such a way that young people can literally experience the movements and transformative encounters proclaimed in the stories. Here we return to the overall intent to plan, construct, and animate sacred space, specifically designed to place young people in a biblical story wherein they are the ones clothed by God, the ones who step out of a boat, the ones who carry the fear and pain that leads to wrestling with an angel, the ones who embrace Esau and build an altar, the ones who climb a tree as they long to encounter Jesus, the ones who eat slop and then return home to embrace their loving parents, the ones who are accused by others, and the ones who encounter those who are accused and affirm their salvific beauty in imitation of Jesus.

Strategically, by opening a Bible story and reflecting on all its powerful elements, we have already discovered ways to insert our young people into its most transformational moment. In fact, in animating a Bible story, there is practically little that can be added to the ingredients already presented throughout this chapter. Here, we add three points of emphasis:

• *Step into the encounter (three-part movement).* Dedicate the bulk of your creativity, time, and resources in service of the powerful journey that moves from suffering, to transformational encounter, to new possibilities. The goal is to place young people physically in the salvific epicenter of the story. A primary way to animate the story's powerful encounter is with music.

In animating the story of the accused woman, we spent a great deal of time creating the soundtrack. We made sure that the music carried the sharp contrast between the angry emotion of the crowd and the serene intimate encounter between Jesus and the woman. Using sound effects and music from the movie soundtrack *Glory* and from Mozart, we moved back and forth from one track to the other, with the crowd standing frozen each time Jesus stooped down to be near the woman.

At a critical moment in the story, the noise from the crowd and the soundtrack abruptly go silent, as Jesus stands up and yells, "Stop," at the crowd. This powerful moment is punctuated by his words, "Let any one of you who is without sin be the first to throw a stone at her." In silence, the crowd turns away from the woman and freezes, followed by the return of the serene music as Jesus again stoops down to be with the woman, who is covered with shame words written on post-it notes.

With the divine music continuing, we inserted young people into this transformational moment as a way for them to share in the salvific actions demonstrated by Jesus. One by one, each young person stood up, walked over to the woman, removed a shame word posted on her body, replaced it with a loving post-it note taken from their own body (symbolizing what they imagined Jesus wrote in the dirt), and whispered affirming words into her ear. (The *loving* and *shame* post-it notes were created earlier by the youth during the asking-questions process.) After the ritual, we spent time foregrounding the issue of bullying recognized by the team and the youth as part of the story connected to their lives. We then reshaped the story into a Starbucks scene to emphasize cyberbullying.

This example demonstrates the impact that music, symbolism, and bodily actions hold in animating the transformational encounters in biblical stories. It also represents the ways in which young people themselves bring the story to life, by including what they had imagined into the ritual (via the post-it notes). By creating a process, which included preliminary exercises and the ritual itself, an imaginative and bodily communion between young people and the salvific life of the story became real.

• *Don't be too literal (expand sacred space)*. While reenactments may contribute to the animation of the story, pastoral leaders should move away from literal reenactments, especially if young people are not inserted into the story. For example, in animating the story of Jacob and Esau, we built an entire journey that utilized most of the pathways and rooms at the Diocese of Fresno youth retreat center. To animate God commanding Jacob to return home, we propped a canopy tent along a path and placed dozens of cell phones inside. As each group entered, a phone rang. After finding the right phone, they answered the call. It was God telling them to return home.

The ritual experience then continued through a long path that each youth traveled alone. The intent of the path was to create an experience like that of Jacob, who carried the weight of his fear and anguish over his broken relationship with his brother. To physically animate this, each young person carried a backpack and encountered a series of drawings with signs that prompted them to pick up a heavy rock and carry it with them. For example, several of the signs along the path read, "We are your mom and your dad. At times we failed you, let you down, and hurt you. And at times, too many times, you still feel the pain of our failures. Take one rock and continue your journey"; "I was your best friend. I stabbed you in the back and we are no longer friends. And at times, too many times, you still grow angry and hurt when thinking of me. Take one rock and continue your journey"; "I am your ex. I shamed you. I used you. I left you. And at times, too many times, you feel your hatred of me in your gut. Take one rock and continue your journey"; and "I am your God. At times, you feel I have abandoned you. Other times, you think I don't care about you. Take one rock and continue on your journey."

Along this path and amid these signs, we placed a six-foot cross with a sign reading,

I am your God. I created you out of love and I am always with you. *"I will heal your broken heart and bind up your wounds."* (see Ps 147:3)

159

After traveling this long path alone, at the end of the trail each youth then encountered one last object—a punching bag with a sign reading, "Use if needed."

Carrying the weight of their broken relationships, the journey continued to the dining hall where a WWE-style wrestling match was about to take place. The match was between the Dark Shadow and the Amazing Jacob. In effect, this was a play inside a play, which involved a soundtrack with music and voice-over, set design, costumes, and performers. Many of the youth were spontaneously able to join in the scene as the Dark Shadow transformed into an angel that wrestled with Jacob all night long and eventually blessed him, giving him hope in continuing his journey. Afterward, the rocks the young people carried were used by them to create an altar.

These examples represent what it means to forego literal reenactments and draw from our creativity inspired by the human emotions and transformative encounters alive in powerful biblical stories. Surprisingly, carrying the weight had a profound impact, and many times afterward, youth groups asked us to re-create the path, including the drawings, signs, rocks, cross, punching bag, and altar (to be filled with the rocks), to be used by their group in the experiences they have created.

• *Emphasize the three-part movement by creating physical movement.* Bodily actions and physical movements are central to animating the salvific essence alive in biblical stories. This, of course, is powerfully evident in the two previous ritual examples. As another example, in animating the story of Creation/fall, we created a winding garden path that led to a dark room, which symbolized the experience of God searching for us when we are lost. With heavy black fabric hovering several feet over the entire floor, upon entering the dark room each young person needed to crawl through the dark room in hope of finding the exit. While trying to find it, two hidden youth leaders standing on ladders swirled flashlights back and forth through the fabric to resemble searchlights. As that happened, a soundtrack (with a male and female voice) was heard in the room repeating the worried question, "Where are you?"

The Animation of Sacred Space

Finding their way through this room, the journey continued through a maze of carnival mirrors physically representing the distorted self-image represented in the following questions that were posted on the mirrors: "Who told you, you were naked?" "Who told you to be ashamed of who you are?" "Who told you to be afraid of Me?" "Who told you that you needed to hide from Me?" "Who told you to only trust yourself?" "Who told you that I am not the deepest part of you?"

At the end of the maze, the scene moved from darkness to light upon hearing God's voice say, "Who told you all this? That did not come from Me. But since your nakedness brings you fear and shame, which makes you want to hide from Me, I will make you clothes so that you will know—I am always with you." Posted on the wall was a large sign stating, "So God made tunics of skin for the man and the woman and clothed them" (see Gen 3:21).

Upon hearing and seeing this, they entered a room greeted by joyful music and a smiling God. God called each by name, wrapped a white blanket around each, and turned each toward a large clear mirror saying, "With me by your side, can you now see the beautiful person that you are?"

After crawling through darkness and seeing distortions of who they are, this encounter brought touch, sight, human interaction, and the warmth of a blanket symbolizing God's unending love and care for them. As a powerful symbol, the blanket reappeared throughout the year and was added to *The Boat* ritual. There, you recall, parents and family members painted their handprints on the blanket, which they then used to wrap around their daughter/son after calling her/his name to step out of the boat. In doing this, we continued the narrative of God making clothes by highlighting ways in which God and loved ones clothe and accompany our young people throughout their lives.

Ultimately, by animating ritual experiences based on Bible stories, pastoral leaders facilitate an encounter with Beauty. Through animation, we engage all the senses and invite bodily movement and actions, trusting that the body has its own way of holding truth and salvific meaning. God wants something from our young people, and while we don't necessarily know the specific nature of it, like Eli, we teach them to respond by having them respond from within the biblical stories we animate: by stepping out of a boat, crawling through a make-shift birth canal, converting rocks into an altar, replacing shame words with loving words, and by navigating a challenging maze in order to end up seeing their true selves clothed by God. Finally, what we build rests upon the word of God and stands in communion with the generations, the love of the faith community, the salvific nature that lives in each young person, and our own salvific personhood.

Hopefully, these twelve strategies representing a narrative approach to ministry have raised awareness of something familiar and known to all of us, which has occurred in our lives in bits and pieces and in the back-and-forth dynamic that defines our relationship with God. In presenting this narrative approach, I have simply attempted for us to see this salvific reality alive in all humanness and give it context and texture in such a way that we can integrate it into the meaning and function of ministry.

Just as ministry mirrors daily human life, we must also realize that ministry cannot facilitate a clean trajectory toward salvific communion, but moves back and forth, and appears and disappears in our efforts to uncover and nurture the salvific narratives in the lives of the youth in our communities.

The same is also true for these twelve strategies, as they, too, are not a linear step-by-step program, but a resemblance of, and testament to, the beautiful salvific process alive in the people we long to serve.

Finally, I am reminded of my favorite Bible verse: "Remain in me, as I also remain in you" (John 15:4 NIV). This has been my holler throughout these pages—GOD IS HERE, alive in our young people. Our continued work as pastoral leaders nurturing this grand narrative, walking alongside our young people, and developing their salvific narratives toward their deepest selves born through generations, animated in communal space, and made real by a God who is always with us and for us.

Notes

Part I: Narrative and Salvation in Ministry

2. Proposing a Narrative Approach to Ministry with Young People

1. Roughhousing is another way to describe this type of fighting, which is considered by some psychotherapists as beneficial to a young person's development. See Theresa Borchard, "6 Benefits of Roughhousing for Kids," *Psych Central* (2013), accessed September 17, 2018, http://psychcentral.com/lib/6-benefits-of-roughhousing-for-kids/; Anthony T. DeBenedet and Lawrence J. Cohen, *The Art of Roughhousing: Good Old-Fashioned Horseplay and Why Every Kid Needs It* (Philadelphia, PA: Quirk Books, 2010).

2. In developing a narrative approach, I am indebted to Paulo Freire's work, in particular his development of *concientización*. See Paulo Freire, *Pedagogy of the Oppressed* (New York: Continuum, 1970), 90–105; Paulo Freire, *Education for Critical Consciousness* (New York: Continuum, 1974), 37–52.

3. This became the focus of my doctoral work. See Vincent A. Olea, "Out of *Cariño*: Fighting and the Embodied Narrative of Inner-City U.S. Hispanic Youth in East Los Angeles" (DMin diss., Barry University, 2014).

4. Regarding poverty, violence, respect, and shame, see "The Alienation Narratives," accessed September 17, 2018, https://www.ctr4ce.com/pages/bidss. See also James Gilligan, *Violence: Reflections on a National Epidemic* (New York: Vintage Books, 1996).

5. See Vincent A. Olea, "Cariño-Fighting and the Somatic Nature of Salvation between Generations" (2016), accessed September 17, 2018, https://ushm.atavist.com/carino-fighting.

6. *See-Judge-Act* is a process intended to engage and understand the daily life of a community (*See*). From that engagement, themes emerge and challenges are named, which require deeper understanding and reflection, leading to a dialogue between the community's life experiences and Sacred Scripture, Christian tradition and theological ideas (*Judge*). With new insights gained from the dialogue, the process provokes a new praxis by and for the community, that is, a new way of interaction that brings about personal and community transformation (*Act*); This historic method is promoted by *Encuentro & Mission* as "relevant, timely, and effective." USCCB, *Encuentro & Mission: A Renewed Pastoral Framework for Hispanic Ministry* (Washington, DC: USCCB, 2002), §21.

3. The Salvific Nature of Being Human

1. Meister Eckhart, *Meister Eckhart: The Essential Sermons, Commentaries, Treatises, and Defense* (Mahwah, NJ: Paulist Press, 1981), 152.

2. Catherine Mowry LaCugna, *God for Us: The Trinity and Christian Life* (San Francisco: HarperCollins, 1991).

3. LaCugna, *God for Us*, 228.

4. LaCugna, *God for Us*, 168.

5. LaCugna, *God for Us*, 228 (Italics in the original).

6. Dietrich Bonhoeffer, *Creation and Fall Temptation: Two Biblical Studies* (New York: Simon & Schuster, 1955), 50.

7. Claus Westermann, *Genesis 1–11: A Continental Commentary*, trans. John J. Scullion, SJ (Minneapolis: Fortress Press, 1994), 206.

8. Westermann, *Genesis 1–11*, 225.

9. An interesting translation offered by the Ancient Hebrew Research Center translates *alone* as "the base word is *bahd/vahd* meaning a 'stick.' The (le) is a prefix meaning 'to' and the (o) is a suffix meaning 'his.' So, *le'vahdo* means 'to his stick.' A stick is a piece of a tree that is separated from the tree. The phrase 'to his stick' is a Hebrew idiom meaning to be 'alone.'" Jeff A. Benner, "Question of the Month," Ancient Hebrew Research Center,

Biblical Hebrew E-Magazine 62 (December 2011). See http://www
.ancient-hebrew.org/emagazine/062.html (accessed June 7, 2018).

10. Phyllis Trible, *God and the Rhetoric of Sexuality* (Philadelphia: Fortress Press, 1978), 89.

11. Here I employ *aloneness* as an umbrella term representing human experiences of separation or isolation, otherwise described as alienation, exile, rejection, heartache, brokenness, hiding, loss, grief, death, abandonment, and the like.

12. Trible, *God and the Rhetoric of Sexuality*, 90.

13. Trible, *God and the Rhetoric of Sexuality*, 99.

14. Westermann, *Genesis 1–11*, 233.

15. Roberto Goizueta, *Caminemos Con Jesús: Toward a Hispanic/Latino Theology of Accompaniment* (New York: Orbis Books, 1995), 130.

16. Regarding *dance*, Miguel Díaz writes, "In this sense, we can metaphorically speak of the human and the divine as being caught up in an eternal nuptial dance in which God is always initiating." Miguel Díaz, *On Being Human: U.S. Hispanic and Rahnerian Perspectives* (New York: Orbis Books, 2001), 24. Ada María Isasi-Díaz writes, "Spirituality is our dance with God, but we cannot dance with God alone. To dance with God we have to bring others." Ada María Isasi-Díaz, *La Lucha Continues: Mujerista Theology* (New York: Orbis Books, 2004), 29.

17. Julian of Norwich, *Showings*, trans. Edmund Colledge, OSA, and James Walsh, SJ (Mahwah, NJ: Paulist Press, 1978), 183.

18. Ronald Rolheiser, *The Holy Longing* (New York: Doubleday, 1999), 4–5.

Part II: Salvific Narratives in the Lives of Hispanic Young People

1. Justice Sonia Sotomayor, "Bill Schuette v. Coalition to Defend Affirmative Action," Dissenting Opinion (April 22, 2014), 46, available online at https://supreme.justia.com/cases/federal/us/572/12-682/dissent7.html (accessed September 19, 2018).

4. The Identity Narratives

1. "The streets" is a common identification for many young people in this area.

2. For more on the "in-between" life, see "The Language Narratives" in chap. 6.

3. Seth J. Schwartz, Jennifer B. Unger, Byron L. Zamboanga, and José Szapocznik, "Rethinking the Concept of Acculturation: Implications for Theory and Research," *The American Psychologist* 65, no. 4 (2010): 237–51, http://www.ncbi.nlm.nih.gov/pmc/articles/PMC3700543/.

4. Gabriel P. Kuperminc, Natalie J. Wilkins, Cathy Roche, and Anabel Alverez-Jimenez, "Risk, Resilience, and Positive Development among Latino Youth," in *Handbook of U.S. Latino Psychology: Developmental and Community-Based Perspectives*, ed. Francisco A. Villarruel, Gustavo Carlo et al. (Los Angeles: Sage, 2009), 222–23.

5. Kuperminc et al., "Risk, Resilience, and Positive Development," 218.

6. Sociologists Roberto Gonzales and Leo Chavez describe it: "The 1.5 generation [consists of] those who migrated at a young age, in recognition of the fact that most or all of their schooling and much of their cultural and social development occur in the host country." Roberto G. Gonzales and Leo R. Chavez, "Awakening to a Nightmare: Abjectivity and Illegality of Undocumented 1.5-Generation Latino Immigrants in the United States," *Current Anthropology* 53, no. 3 (2012): 257–58.

7. Migration Policy Institute data tabulation from the U.S. Census Bureau's 2010 and 2014 American Community Surveys and 2000 Decennial Census: Jie Zong, Jeanne Batalova, and Jeffrey Hallock, "Frequently Requested Statistics on Immigrants and Immigration in the U.S," *Migration Policy Institute*, April 14, 2016, http://www.migrationpolicy.org/article/frequently-requested-statistics-immigrants-and-immigration-united-states?gclid=CPWcpMzhus4CFU9bfgodyd4How.

8. Renee Stepler and Anna Brown, "Facts on U.S. Latinos, 2015: Statistical Portrait of Hispanics in the United States," *Pew Research Center, Hispanic Trends*, April 19, 2016, http://www.pewhispanic.org/2016/04/19/statistical-portrait-of-hispanics-in-the-united-states-key-charts/.

9. Jens Manuel Krogstad and Gustavo López, "Roughly Half of Hispanics Have Experienced Discrimination," *Pew Research Center, Fact Tank,* June 29, 2016, http://www.pewresearch.org/fact-tank/2016/06/29/roughly-half-of-hispanics-have-experienced-discrimination/.

10. Jens Manuel Krogstad and Gustavo López, "Roughly Half of Hispanics Have Experienced Discrimination."

11. Kuperminc et al., "Risk, Resilience, and Positive Development," 224.

12. See "The Language Narratives" in chap. 6.

13. Kuperminc et al., "Risk, Resilience, and Positive Development," 223.

14. Pew Research Center: Religion and Public Life Project, "The Shifting Religious Identity of Latinos in the United States: Nearly One-in-Four Latinos are Former Catholics," May 7, 2014, http://www.pewforum.org/2014/05/07/the-shifting-religious-identity-of-latinos-in-the-united-states/.

15. Hosffman Ospino, "American and Catholic in an Increasingly Catholic Church," *C21 Resources* (Spring 2016): 3–4.

16. This important narrative theme and the experiences of religious disengagement are discussed in more detail in "The Generational Narratives" (chap. 5) and "The Animation of Sacred Space" (chap. 10).

5. THE GENERATIONAL NARRATIVES

1. Virgilio Elizondo, *Galilean Journey: The Mexican-American Promise* (New York: Orbis Books, 1983), 7–23; Allan Figueroa Deck, *The Second Wave: Hispanic Ministry and the Evangelization of Cultures* (New York: Paulist Press, 1989), 26–53; The United States also engaged in the conquest of Mexico (1845–48), contributing to the oppressive history of a people.

2. Elizondo, *Galilean Journey,* 7–8.

3. Roberto Goizueta, *Christ Our Companion: Toward a Theological Aesthetics of Liberation* (New York: Maryknoll, 2009), 21.

4. Recent examples include the following: the 1943 Zoot Suit Riots; Operation Wetback in 1954, which enacted mass deportation of nearly 3 million Latin Americans; the creation of the United Farm Workers in 1962 by Cesar Chavez and Dolores

Huerta in response to the abhorrent treatment and conditions of farm workers; the 1968 Los Angeles student Walkout in response to unequal treatment including punishment for speaking Spanish and removal of bathroom usage during lunch; California proposition 187 (1994–95), prohibiting undocumented Latinos from health care, public education, and public services (1997, ruled unconstitutional); 2016 expiration of the Voter Rights Act; and the 2017 attempt to terminate DACA (Deferred Action for Childhood Arrivals) by the Trump Administration. The range of harmful effects related to poverty and discriminatory systems today is explored in "The Alienation Narratives" available online at https://www.ctr4ce.com/pages/bidss.

5. Examples of these studies include the following: Karina Walters, Selina A. Mohammed et al., "Bodies Don't Just Tell Stories, They Tell Histories: Embodiment of Historical Trauma among American Indians and Alaska Natives," *Du Bois Review* 8, no. 1 (2011): 179–89; Michael Weiss and Sima Weiss, "Second Generation to Holocaust Survivors: Enhanced Differentiation of Trauma Transmission," *American Journal of Psychotherapy* 54, no. 3 (2000): 372–85; Bettye Jean Ford, "Transmission of Generational Trauma in African American Members" (PhD diss., Pacifica Graduate Institute, 2014); Antonio L. Estrada, "Mexican Americans and Historical Trauma Theory: A Theoretical Perspective," *Journal of Ethnicity in Substance Abuse* 8, no. 3 (2009): 330–40.

6. For a concise and accessible understanding of epigenetics, see Dan Hurly, "Grandma's Experiences Leave a Mark on Your Genes," *Discover* (May 2013), accessed September 19, 2018, http://discovermagazine.com/2013/may/13-grandmas-experiences-leave-epigenetic-mark-on-your-genes.

7. Dan Hurly, "Grandma's Experiences Leave a Mark on Your Genes," 3.

8. Laurence J. Kirmayer, Joseph P. Gone, Joshua Moses, "Rethinking Historical Trauma," *Transcultural Psychiatry*, 51, no. 3 (2014): 309.

9. Karina Walters, Selina A. Mohammed, et al. "Bodies Don't Just Tell Stories, They Tell Histories," 186.

10. Jeanette Rodriguez, "Sangre llama a sangre: Cultural Memory as a Source of Theological Insight," in *Hispanic/Latino Theology:*

Challenge and Promise, ed. Ada Maria Isasi-Diaz and Fernando F. Segovia (Minneapolis: Fortress Press, 1996), 122.

11. Rodriguez, "Sangre llama a sangre," 118.

12. For the full narrative, see Virgilio Elizondo, *La Morenita: Evangelizer of the Americas* (San Antonio: MACC Bookstore, 1980), 75–81.

13. Ada María Isasi-Díaz, *La Lucha Continues: Mujerista Theology* (New York: Orbis Books, 2004), 258.

14. Goizueta, *Christ Our Companion*, 144.

15. Miguel Díaz, *On Being Human: U.S. Hispanic and Rahnerian Perspectives* (New York: Orbis Books, 2001), 70.

16. Traditions including *Las Posadas* (reenactment of Mary and Joseph looking for lodging), *Pastorelas* (nativity play), *Nacimientos* (nativity scene), *Nochebuena* (Christmas Eve celebration including opening gifts), and *Día de los Reyes Magos* (January 6 celebration of the Three Kings).

17. For more information about the complexity and challenges of this narrative theme, see "The Animation of Sacred Space" in chap. 10 and "The Somatic Narratives," available online at https://www.ctr4ce.com/pages/bidss.

6. THE LANGUAGE NARRATIVES

1. Roberto Goizueta, *Caminemos Con Jesús: Toward a Hispanic/Latino Theology of Accompaniment* (New York: Orbis Books, 1995), 5–6. Italics in the original.

2. Virgilio Elizondo, *The Future Is Mestizo: Life Where Cultures Meet*, rev. ed. (Boulder, CO: University of Colorado Press, 2000), 17.

3. Ana María Pineda, "Personal and Ministerial Formation in a Hispanic Context," In *Dialogue Rejoined: Theology and Ministry in the United States Hispanic Reality*, ed. Ana María Pineda and Robert Schreiter (Collegeville, MN: Liturgical Press, 1995), 153.

4. Jens Manuel Krogstad and Ana Gonzalez-Barrera, "A Majority of English-Speaking Hispanics in the U.S. Are Bilingual, *Pew Research Center*, March 24, 2015, http://www.pewresearch.org/fact-tank/2015/03/24/a-majority-of-english-speaking-hispanics-in-the-u-s-are-bilingual/.

5. Jorge L. Presmanes, "Bilingual Liturgy: A U.S. Latino Perspective," *Liturgical Ministry* 16 (2007): 142; Embedded quote from Roberto Heredia and Jeanette Altarriba, "Bilingual Language Mixing: Why Do Bilinguals Code-Switch?" *Current Directions in Psychological Science* 10, no. 5 (2001): 164.

6. Presmanes, "Bilingual Liturgy," 142–43.

7. Ada María Isasi Díaz, *En La Lucha, In the Struggle: Elaborating a Mujerista Theology* (Minneapolis: Fortress Press, 1993), 52–53.

8. Miguel Díaz, *On Being Human: U.S. Hispanic and Rahnerian Perspectives* (New York: Orbis Books, 2001), 13.

9. Eileen Patton, "The Nations Latino Population Is Defined by Its Youth," *Pew Research Center, Hispanic Trends*, April 20, 2016, http://www.pewhispanic.org/2016/04/20/the-nations-latino-population-is-defined-by-its-youth/.

10. Jens Manuel Krogstad, "Rise in English Proficiency among U.S. Hispanics Is Driven by the Young," *Pew Research Center*, April 20, 2016, http://www.pewresearch.org/fact-tank/2016/04/20/rise-in-english-proficiency-among-u-s-hispanics-is-driven-by-the-young/.

11. Krogstad, "Rise in English Proficiency among U.S. Hispanics." Note: young Hispanics ages zero to four are not calculated in these statistics.

12. Jens Manuel Krogstad and Ana Gonzalez-Barrera, "A Majority of English Speaking Hispanics in the U.S. Are Bilingual," *Pew Research Center*, March 24, 2015, http://www.pewresearch.org/fact-tank/2015/03/24/a-majority-of-english-speaking-hispanics-in-the-u-s-are-bilingual/.

13. Pew Research Center, "Between Two Worlds: How Young Latinos Come of Age in America," December 11, 2009, 21.

14. Timothy Matovina, *Latino Catholicism: Transformation in America's Largest Church* (Princeton: Princeton University Press, 2012), 221.

15. Matovina, *Latino Catholicism*, 221.

16. Hosffman Ospino, "American and Catholic in an Increasingly Catholic Church," *The Church in the 21st Century Center: A Catalyst and Resource for the Renewal of the Catholic Church* (Spring 2016): 3–4.

17. Pew Research Center: Religion and Public Life Project, "The Shifting Religious Identity of Latinos in the United States: Nearly One-in-Four Latinos Are Former Catholics," May 7, 2014, http://www.pewforum.org/2014/05/07/the-shifting-religious-identity-of-latinos-in-the-united-states/.

18. See "The Somatic Narratives," available online at https://www.ctr4ce.com/pages/bidss.

19. See "The Relationality Narratives," available at https://www.ctr4ce.com/pages/bidss.

7. The Transformative Narratives

1. See "The Relationality Narratives," available online at https://www.ctr4ce.com/pages/bidss.

2. See "The Somatic Narratives," available online at https://www.ctr4ce.com/pages/bidss.

3. Greg Boyle, *Tattoos on the Heart: The Power of Boundless Compassion* (New York: Free Press, 2010).

4. Greg Boyle, *Tattoos on the Heart*, 53–54.

5. Tupac Shakur embraced *Thug Life* considering it a way of life affected by poverty and disenfranchisement. Michael Erik Dyson, *Holler If You Hear Me, Searching for Tupac Shakur* (New York: Basic Civitas Books, 2001), 112–13, 115.

Part III: Practical Strategies for a Narrative Approach to Ministry

8. Strategies to See and Give Voice in a Narrative Approach

1. Antonio Spadaro, "The Exclusive Interview with Pope Francis: A Big Heart Open to God," in *America*, September 30, 2013, 26.

2. For a historical survey of the see-judge-act method, see Ana María Bidegain, "From Catholic Action to Liberation Theology: The Historical Process of the Laity in Latin America in the Twentieth Century," (working paper #48, The Helen Kellogg Institute for International Studies, University of Notre Dame, 1985),

available at https://kellogg.nd.edu/publications/workingpapers/
WPS/048.pdf (accessed September 21, 2018).

3. Roberto Goizueta, *Caminemos Con Jesús: Toward a Hispanic/Latino Theology of Accompaniment* (New York: Orbis Books, 1995), 130.

4. National Catholic Network de Pastoral Juvenil Hispana—La Red, *Primer Encuentro Nacional de Pastoral Juvenil Hispana Conclusiones: Bilingual Edition* (Washington, DC: USCCB, 2008), 57, 11, 34.

5. For an examination of social media and young Hispanics today, see "The Relationality Narratives," available online at https://www.ctr4ce.com/pages/bidss.

6. See "The Somatic Narratives," available online at https://www.ctr4ce.com/pages/bidss.

7. Paulo Freire discusses the "naming of the world" when examining dialogue: Paulo Freire, *Pedagogy of the Oppressed* (New York: Continuum, 1970), 69–70.

9. Bringing Narratives Together by Bringing Lives Together

1. Geffrey B. Kelly, *Karl Rahner: Theologian of the Graced Search for Meaning* (Minneapolis: Fortress Press, 1992), 43.

2. Alejandro García-Rivera, *The Community of the Beautiful: A Theological Aesthetics* (Collegeville, MN: Liturgical Press, 1999), 35.

3. García-Rivera, *The Community of the Beautiful*, 36–37.

4. García-Rivera, *The Community of the Beautiful*, 36.

10. The Animation of Sacred Space

1. Richard Rohr, *Adam's Return: The Five Promises of Male Initiation* (New York: Crossroad Publishing, 2004), 143.

2. Victor Turner, *From Ritual to Theatre: The Human Seriousness of Play* (New York: PAJ Publications, 2001), 80. Italics in the original.

3. Richard Rohr, "A Trinitarian Worldview" (course lecture, Loyola Marymount University: Los Angeles, CA, July 10–13, 2006).